The
Use-It-Up
Cookbook

The
Use-It-Up
Cookbook

CREATIVE RECIPES FOR THE FRUGAL COOK

Catherine Kitcho

Cumberland House
Nashville, Tennessee

For my mother, Mildred Kitcho

Thanks for the cooking genes
and the inspiration!

Copyright © 2003 by Catherine Kitcho

Published by
Cumberland House Publishing
431 Harding Industrial Drive
Nashville, Tennessee 37211
www.cumberlandhouse.com

Cover design: Unlikely Suburban Design
Text design: Mary Sanford

Library of Congress Cataloging-in-Publication Data
Kitcho, Catherine.
  The use-it-up cookbook : creative recipes for the frugal cook /
Catherine Kitcho.
     p. cm.
  ISBN 1-58182-366-5 (pbk. : alk. paper)
  1. Cookery (Leftovers) I. Title.
  TX652.K4686 2003
  641.5'52—dc22
                                                   2003015134

Printed in the United States
1 2 3 4 5 6 7—09 08 07 06 05 04 03

Contents

Acknowledgments

A cookbook project requires many hours in the kitchen during recipe development and many hours at the computer translating those kitchen experiments into effective prose. I have thoroughly enjoyed every one of those hours, but I could not have done it without my team of supporters, tasters, friends, and family encouraging me every step of the way.

To the entire staff of Cumberland House, thank you for believing in my vision for this book. You understood it from the beginning, and your staff has been wonderfully supportive and professional throughout the entire process. It's a pleasure to work with you. To my editor, Mary Sanford, you are just the best! With your guidance, you helped me avoid problems before they became problems.

Thanks to my family and friends who became willing—or not-so-willing—tasters of the experiments along the way, and who provided me with feedback and suggestions for improvement. Thanks to my dear husband, David: although you were often surprised to find out what was for dinner, you tasted it anyway. My niece, Julie Natalini, and her husband, Larry, were also great tasters, as well as my friend Kathy Foist and the staff at Solstice Salon. Thank you for your feedback and your candor in giving me suggestions for making this book even better.

Introduction

The two bananas have become more brown than yellow. You've moved the half-carton of buttermilk in the refrigerator yet again to retrieve something on the shelf behind it. The remainder of the bunch of celery has promise of at least one or two stalks that are still green. And then there's the little can of tomato paste, with a tablespoon of it gone—used in some recipe tonight. The chips are eaten, but there's salsa left. Does this sound like your kitchen?

If you have pent-up guilt about throwing away food, if you were lectured by one or more parents about wasting food, or if you just want to be frugal about using all the food you have paid for, then this is the book for you. Throw out the guilt, and use up what's left of the package, jar, bottle, bunch, or can! In this book you will find original recipes for using up those ingredients.

BORN OF NECESSITY

I've been a cook for more than forty years. I've cooked for my family, my friends, and myself. As a child, I loved helping my mother cook, and I inherited her passion for collecting recipes and cookbooks, as well as her view of cooking as a creative pursuit. When I was in my late thirties, I founded, managed, and then sold a catering company called Five Star Kitchens. My catering company's focus was on healthy, gourmet foods with ethnic themes, such as Mexican, Italian, Russian, Chinese, and even Cajun. I developed the recipes and menus myself, and then converted them for crowd-sized quantities.

With all the cooking experimentation throughout my forty-year history in the kitchen, there was one constant problem: leftover bits of ingredients. (And when I had the catering company, there were larger bits of leftover ingredients!) When the ingredients would pile up in the refrigerator or the pantry, I would start leafing through my ever-growing cookbook collection to find a quick fix—a recipe that would use up what I had left. This exercise was futile, however, because I could never find "buttermilk" or "cooked rice" or "tomato paste" listed in the index or table of contents. That meant I would have to read through the cookbook page by page, hoping to find something, but who has time to do that? I would say to myself, "Why can't there be a cookbook out there that lists these ingredients in the index, or better yet, that is organized by ingredient?" In frustration, I would end up throwing the remainder of the ingredient away, feeling a bit guilty about wasting food. Eventually, I decided to end my frustration and the frustration of other like-minded cooks by writing this book.

Some of these recipes come from my catering days, some are adapted childhood favorites, and the rest were developed specifically for this book. You will find recipes for soups, salads, meat, poultry, fish, desserts, breads, and many other dishes.

C⁓ COOKING STYLE

Over the years, I've adapted my cooking style to include healthier ingredients and cooking methods. These days, I use olive oil for cooking and butter or canola oil for baking. Therefore, you will see olive oil or butter listed in the recipes in this book. You can, of course, substitute whatever cooking oil you prefer to use. I don't deep-fry foods at all anymore, and when I sauté foods, I try to use the least amount of oil possible to accomplish the task or to add enough flavor without overwhelming the food that's being cooked.

With yeast breads, I use instant yeast, adding it to the dry ingredients first and adding liquid later, instead of vice versa. The directions for the bread recipes in this book follow this procedure. That's because I have better results with instant yeast. However, if you prefer, you can proof yeast in water first and then add it to the other dry ingredients in the recipe.

I also tend to reduce the amount of sugar in a recipe when I can, or use other ingredients that add sweetness to the recipe. You may want to try the recipes the first time as is, and if you prefer more sweetness, you can always add a bit more sugar. In cooking, I use skim milk instead of regular milk. This comes from many years of watching my calories! These recipes were all tested with skim milk, but you can use whole or low-fat milk if you wish.

C⁓ HOW TO USE THIS BOOK

The first thing you should do when you open this book is turn to the back! You need to make sure that whatever you want to use up is still safe to cook with, and at the back of the book is an appendix with safe food storage guidelines. Then, assuming what you want to use up is still safe, proceed to the table of contents. *The Use-It-Up Cookbook* is organized into twenty-five chapters, arranged alphabetically by ingredient. Within each chapter, you will find a brief description of the ingredient, followed by five recipes that use the ingredient. Some of the recipes are "2-fers," which use up two of the book's featured ingredients, and a few are even "3-fers." Look for the symbols that indicate these recipes:

The book also provides further inspiration for you to experiment in the kitchen and develop your own recipes. After the recipes in each chapter is a creative guide that describes the ingredient and how to combine it with other tastes, flavors, or textures to enhance its unique properties. Along with the creative guide is plenty of space for you to record your own original recipes for the particular ingredient, along with notes and ideas. I encourage you to try one or two of the recipes in the chapters, and then try some of your own.

At the end of the book you will find the appendix on safe food storage. There are guidelines for storage of all the ingredients featured in the book, as well as links for finding more food safety information on the Internet. At the very end is a list of 2-fers and 3-fers, and the index. And because we finally have a whole book that is already organized by ingredient, this index is organized by type of dish and type of food.

After you've used this book for a while, you may want to keep it handy when you plan meals and write out your grocery lists. That way, you will buy all the items needed to cook your meals and use up all the ingredients at the same time.

ᴄ CREATIVE FRUGALITY

I hope you enjoy these recipes and that you will be inspired to develop even more fabulous dishes that use up these ingredients. As you exercise your creativity, I hope that you also feel good about not wasting food and getting the most out of every food dollar. May all of your creative cooking endeavors be wildly successful, and remember to have fun!

Catherine Kitcho
May 2003

The
Use-It-Up
Cookbook

1
Applesauce

The original applesauce was made out of necessity: to preserve an overabundant harvest from the apple orchard. Women cooked and canned applesauce for years, to enjoy throughout the winter and spring until the next harvest. Today, commercially prepared applesauce is a whole product category, packaged in single-serving cups or one-pint jars, flavored with cinnamon or sugar or berries, or au naturel. Regardless of how it's packaged, there will probably come a day when your family tires of eating it plain, and it's time to figure out what to do with the rest. Unsweetened applesauce is my preference, because I think it tastes most like a real apple, and that's what I use in recipes.

Apple pectin is a good source of fiber, so adding it to recipes will provide moisture and thickening without adding an overpowering flavor. The following recipes highlight the unique texture and delicate flavor of applesauce.

Saucy Coleslaw

It's becoming more difficult to find bottled coleslaw dressing in the supermarket these days. This simple and easy recipe is a great alternative, with the right balance of tartness and sweetness to enhance the flavor of the cabbage. Applesauce lends sweetness and body, resulting in the right consistency to coat the cabbage and add flavor.

½ cup applesauce
½ cup mayonnaise
¼ teaspoon onion powder
¼ teaspoon celery salt
1 teaspoon prepared mustard
1 teaspoon sugar
2 tablespoons water
4 cups shredded cabbage or packaged coleslaw mix

In a large mixing bowl combine the applesauce and mayonnaise. Blend with a wire whisk until all the mayonnaise lumps are gone. Add the spices, mustard, sugar, and water, and blend until smooth. Add the cabbage or coleslaw mix and stir until well coated. Refrigerate for several hours or overnight so that the flavors penetrate the cabbage. Makes 4 to 8 servings.

2 tablespoons butter

⅓ cup sugar

1 egg

⅓ cup milk

⅓ cup applesauce

½ teaspoon butter flavoring

½ teaspoon vanilla

1⅓ cups all-purpose flour

2 teaspoons baking powder

¼ teaspoon salt

Topping:

¼ cup applesauce

¼ cup chopped pecans

¼ cup caramel ice cream topping (or caramel dip)

Caramel Apple Brownies

I used to love caramel apples when I was a kid. Biting through the luscious caramel and tasting the tart apple underneath was a delightful contrast in flavors and textures. For those of you who love that combination, these brownies will help recall those childhood memories.

Preheat the oven to 350°. Brush an 8-inch square baking pan with oil or spray with cooking spray. In a large mixing bowl cream together the butter and sugar until blended; add the egg, milk, applesauce, butter flavoring, and vanilla and blend thoroughly. In a separate bowl mix together the flour, baking powder, and salt, then add to the wet mixture. Mix thoroughly again until the batter is smooth. Pour into the prepared pan and smooth with a spatula. With a spoon scatter dabs of applesauce evenly over the batter, and then sprinkle the chopped pecans over the batter. Spoon the caramel topping over, then swirl the caramel with a spoon until well distributed. Bake for 30 minutes. Let cool, then cut into bars. Makes 12 to 16 brownies.

Appleberry Breakfast Crepes

My mother made crepes for us on a regular basis, and we liked them better than pancakes. Crepes are lighter and more delicate, and can be filled with many different things: fruits, ricotta or cream cheese, even meats or poultry. For a wonderful weekend breakfast or brunch, try these festive crepes. The applesauce provides a delicate and sweet background for the berries. Use whatever berries are in season, such as raspberries, blueberries, or blackberries. Save some berries to sprinkle over the top of the crepes when you serve them.

2	eggs
½	cup all-purpose flour
⅛	teaspoon salt
½	cup milk
1	tablespoon melted butter

Filling:
  Applesauce
  Fresh berries

Using an electric mixer or a stand mixer, beat the eggs thoroughly. Add the flour, salt, milk, and butter. Blend thoroughly. To cook the crepes, use a pancake griddle, crepe pan, or small frying pan. Heat the pan or griddle to medium high heat. Pour ¼ to ⅓ cup batter into the pan or onto the griddle. Allow the crepes to cook until bubbles form on top, then flip over and brown for 1 to 2 more minutes. Remove to a platter until all crepes are cooked.

Place the crepes on a flat surface, and spoon 1 to 2 tablespoons of applesauce inside, then sprinkle with a few berries. Roll up and then place seam side down on a serving platter. You can warm them in a preheated oven or microwave them for a few minutes on low if you want to serve them warm. Makes 6 crepes; double the recipe if you are serving more people.

4½ cups all-purpose flour
½ cup brown sugar
¼ teaspoon salt
½ teaspoon baking soda
1 teaspoon cinnamon
1 tablespoon instant yeast
1 cup water
2 tablespoons butter
1 egg
½ cup applesauce

Filling:
1 tablespoon melted butter
1 teaspoon cinnamon
2 tablespoons brown sugar
  Nuts or raisins as desired

Apple Cinnamon Rolls

Cinnamon rolls are one of my all-time favorite foods—any time of the day or night. I like a moist cinnamon roll, and adding applesauce to the dough really gives the rolls a nice texture, along with a hint of sweetness. You can vary the filling depending on your own tastes: some people like nuts and raisins, some don't. These keep pretty well, but you might want to refrigerate them; the extra moisture may promote mold.

In a large bowl mix 3 cups flour, the brown sugar, salt, soda, cinnamon, and yeast. In a small saucepan heat the water and butter until the temperature is about 105°, then add to the dry ingredients and beat well. Add the egg and applesauce, and mix until blended. Gradually add flour until the mixture cleans the bowl. Turn out onto a floured board and knead for about 5 minutes, adding more of the remaining flour as needed until the dough is elastic. Cover and let rise in a warm place until doubled.

Preheat the oven to 375°. Grease a 9 x 13-inch baking pan. When the dough has risen, punch it down and roll it out onto a floured board into a 10 x 14-inch rectangle. Brush the melted butter over the dough, then sprinkle with cinnamon and brown sugar. Sprinkle nuts or raisins over the dough as desired. Roll into a log, sealing the edge. Cut into 12 1-inch slices. Place in the prepared pan. Let rise again for about 20 minutes until doubled. Bake for 20 minutes. Frost with powdered sugar frosting if desired. Makes 12 large rolls.

Apple Walnut Cheesecake

The crunch of walnuts and the subtle tartness of applesauce in this cheesecake make it perfect for fall. Applesauce adds bulk to the cheesecake, so in effect it replaces one package of cream cheese that you would otherwise use.

On a baking sheet toast the walnuts in a 350° oven for 10 minutes; set aside. Reduce the oven temperature to 325°. Lightly brush an 8½-inch springform pan with cooking oil. In a saucepan or the microwave melt the butter and mix it with the graham cracker crumbs; press into the bottom of the pan.

Using a blender purée the applesauce until it is very smooth and creamy with no lumps remaining. Add the ricotta cheese and blend again until very smooth. Add the cream cheese, eggs, sugar, cinnamon, vanilla, and lemon juice, and blend well. Transfer the mixture to a mixing bowl and stir in the walnuts gently. Pour the mixture into the prepared pan. Bake for 1 hour. Turn off the oven, leaving the door ajar. Let the cheesecake cool in the oven for 1 hour. Makes 12 servings.

½	cup chopped walnuts
1	tablespoon butter
½	cup graham cracker crumbs
1	cup applesauce
1	15-ounce carton ricotta cheese
1	8-ounce package cream cheese
4	eggs
⅔	cup sugar
1	teaspoon cinnamon
1	teaspoon vanilla
1	teaspoon lemon juice

Also uses eggs

The flavor of applesauce is delicate and subtle, so it needs contrasting tart or spicy flavors in the recipe. Cinnamon and nutmeg are the most common spices used with applesauce, but you can also try cloves, coriander, or anise for a unique taste. Applesauce added to baked goods will add moisture and yield a slightly heavier crumb. When added to otherwise smooth ingredients, applesauce can sometimes be gritty. To reduce the grittiness, try putting it through a blender first (as in the cheesecake recipe). Buttery and sweet flavors go well with applesauce (think of apple pie). Try adding applesauce to smoothies, gelatin, or homemade ice cream to add richness without adding calories.

NOTES

From the kitchen of ——————

From the kitchen of ——————

2
Bananas

As one of the most popular fruits, bananas are found in nearly every kitchen. Banana eaters are very particular about the perfect point of ripeness to suit their tastes. I enjoy bananas when they are still yellow, just barely past the green stage. If there's the slightest hint of brown, I'd rather cook with them than eat them plain. Other people are just the opposite, and prefer them when they are riper and sweeter. Quite often, bananas hang around until they are well past the point of enjoyable eating by anyone, and that's usually when the banana bread recipe is dragged out once again. However, there is more to do with leftover ripe bananas than just make banana bread. Bananas' sweetness and texture enhance other types of baked goods, and when frozen, they can be transformed into a luscious sorbet. Here are some new ways to use this marvelous and healthful fruit.

Caribbean Sorbet

1	banana per person
1	tablespoon rum per person
	Ground nutmeg for garnish

This is one of the simplest and most elegant desserts I have ever served to dinner guests, and it always gets rave reviews. If they only knew they were eating leftover frozen bananas (dressed up a bit, of course)! Because the bananas need to be solidly frozen to make this dessert, it's a good idea to always have some in your freezer ready to go.

When your bananas start to turn brown, peel them and wrap them individually in heavy plastic wrap. (*Note:* Don't freeze them in the peel because it's too difficult to get the peel off.) About 15 minutes before you want to serve dessert, remove the bananas from the freezer. Unwrap and slice into chunks with a sharp knife. Place the banana chunks into a food processor or blender and add the rum. Process (cover your ears—it will make quite a racket) until the bananas are smooth like ice cream. Spoon the mixture into large wine goblets or crystal dessert dishes, and sprinkle a little nutmeg on top before serving. For a nonalcoholic version, you can replace the rum with ½ teaspoon of rum extract per banana.

2¼ cups all-purpose flour
2   teaspoons baking
    powder
¼   teaspoon soda
½   teaspoon salt
3   medium bananas
½   cup butter
¾   cup sugar
3   1-ounce squares
    semisweet chocolate,
    melted
2   eggs
1   teaspoon vanilla
½   cup chopped nuts
    (pecans, walnuts,
    almonds)

Chocobanana Bars

My mother used to make a soft chocolate cookie with bananas and walnuts. I adapted the recipe so that it's more of a cake-like brownie. Chocolate and banana make a great flavor combination, and adding nuts, such as pecans or walnuts, adds a little bit of crunch. You could also add some coconut for a more tropical taste.

Preheat the oven to 375°. Grease a 9 x 13-inch pan. In a large bowl mix together the flour, baking powder, soda, and salt. In a food processor or blender mash the bananas. Add the butter and sugar, and continue processing until smooth. Add the chocolate, eggs, and vanilla, and blend until smooth. Pour over the dry ingredients and stir until smooth. Stir in the nuts until evenly distributed. Pour into the prepared pan. Bake for 30 minutes or until done in the center. Makes 36 brownies.

Tropical Delight Muffins

Adding bananas to a muffin recipe not only adds a unique flavor, but also adds sweetness so that you can reduce the amount of sugar in the recipe. This muffin recipe uses oatmeal, which gives the muffins more body and also adds healthy fiber. Try substituting some of the flour with whole wheat or brown rice flour for another variation. To make them more tropical, add ¼ cup crushed pineapple.

Preheat the oven to 375°. Grease the tins of a muffin pan or line with paper muffin cups. In a large bowl blend together the eggs, brown sugar, oil, and milk using an electric mixer. Mash the bananas and add to the mixture; blend again. In a separate large mixing bowl blend together the rolled oats, flour, baking powder, soda, and salt. Stir in the coconut. Pour the wet ingredients over the dry ingredients, stirring just until the lumps are gone. Bake for 22 minutes. Let cool in the pan for 10 minutes, then transfer to a cooling rack. Makes 12 muffins.

2	eggs
⅓	cup brown sugar
½	cup vegetable oil
¼	cup milk
2	ripe bananas
1	cup old-fashioned rolled oats
1½	cups all-purpose flour
1	tablespoon baking powder
½	teaspoon baking soda
½	teaspoon salt
¼	cup unsweetened shredded coconut

½   cup all-purpose flour
    Dash salt
¼   teaspoon baking soda
½   teaspoon baking
    powder
½   cup peanut butter
¼   cup softened butter
2   medium bananas
½   cup sugar
1   teaspoon vanilla
2   eggs
½   cup walnuts or pecans

PBB Brownies

When I was a kid, I used to take two slices of my mother's homemade bread, spread them with peanut butter, and put slices of banana in the middle. That was my after-school snack, or sometimes, that was breakfast! I still love that combination of peanut butter and bananas (PBB), and developed this brownie recipe that combines those flavors. If you are allergic to peanuts, try making this with almond butter instead.

Preheat the oven to 350°. Grease an 8-inch square pan or coat with cooking spray. In a small mixing bowl blend together the flour, salt, soda, and baking powder. Using a mixer or a food processor, blend together the peanut butter and butter until smooth. Mash the bananas and add to the peanut butter mixture along with the sugar, vanilla, and eggs. Mix well until the batter is smooth. Add the dry ingredients and mix until smooth. Add the walnuts or pecans and mix until well distributed. Bake for 25 to 30 minutes or until done in the center. Makes 12 to 16 brownies.

David's Pancakes

My husband, David, is the master pancake chef in our family. He has the magic touch when it comes to this classic breakfast food; I, alas, do not. This recipe has evolved over the years, and he has varied the types of flour, beat the egg whites separately or not, and added other fruits or not. But whatever the variation, bananas are always the primary sweetener in this recipe. If you've never cooked with brown rice flour, you should try it. It makes the pancakes light, delicate, and just plain delicious.

In a large mixing bowl blend the flour, baking powder, and flaxseed. (*Note:* Flaxseed thickens the pancakes; so if you don't use it, reduce the milk by ¼ cup.) In a smaller mixing bowl whisk together the milk, oil, and eggs, then add to the dry ingredients. Mix until well blended with no lumps remaining. In a blender or food processor purée the bananas and add to the batter. Stir in the blueberries. Heat the griddle to 350°. Cook on the first side until bubbles form at the top and the pancakes look dry at the edges. Flip them over and cook until both sides are brown, 1 to 2 minutes more. Makes 18 pancakes, 4 inches in diameter.

2	cups brown rice flour or combination (1 cup brown rice flour, ½ cup cornmeal, ¾ cup rolled oats ground in blender)
1	tablespoon baking powder
3	tablespoons flaxseed, ground (optional—see note at left)
2	cups milk
¼	cup canola oil
3	eggs
2	or 3 ripe bananas
½	to 1 cup blueberries

Also uses eggs

Bananas are a great substitute for sugar in some recipes, reducing calories and providing more nutrition. You'll need to mash the bananas or put them in a blender or food processor until smooth, then add the bananas to the recipe along with the other wet ingredients. Try replacing sugar with bananas at the ratio of 1 banana = ¼ cup sugar. Also keep in mind that bananas do have a distinct taste that will come through in the baked goods, and the taste can overpower the other flavors in the recipe. Bananas added to baked goods will add more bulk and more moisture, so the result will be a heavier and chewier crumb. The flavor of bananas contrasts well with chocolate, and nuts such as almonds, peanuts, walnuts, and pecans. Other tropical flavors, such as pineapple, coconut, and mango, also work well with bananas. When frozen, bananas have a smooth, ice-cream-like texture, which can form a great base for smoothies, also. Hot or cold, bananas are a very versatile fruit to have around the kitchen.

2 for For more recipes that use up bananas, see:

Jamuffins, p. 83

NOTES

_____
_____
_____
_____
_____
_____
_____
_____

From the kitchen of

From the kitchen of

3

Bread

In today's supermarkets there are so many different varieties and flavors of bread that it's hard to choose. The average household has more than one type of loaf in the kitchen at any given time; some for toasting, some for sandwiches, and a crusty loaf to dip in olive oil or serve with pasta. Because of this abundance and variety, portions of loaves are often left over. Even bread with preservatives will tend to dry out and taste stale. You can extend the shelf life of bread by keeping it in the refrigerator, but that tends to dry it out as well, and it can also lose flavor. So it's time to do something else with it! You can use leftover bread as is, let it dry at room temperature and then use it in recipes, or dry it and make it into breadcrumbs. The recipes in this chapter will work for white bread, whole grain breads, or rye bread. You can also use thin-sliced, low-calorie bread for a lower-calorie version of these dishes.

Bread Salad

Don't be fooled by the strange title of this recipe; it's really great, especially made with freshly picked ripe tomatoes and fresh basil. It makes a wonderful accompaniment to grilled chicken, fish, or Italian sausage.

4	slices Italian or crusty French bread, toasted lightly
4	small ripe Roma or salad tomatoes
8	leaves fresh basil
2	green onions, chopped
¼	cup vinaigrette salad dressing

Cut the toasted bread slices into 1-inch squares and place in a mixing bowl. Dice the fresh tomatoes and add to the bowl. Mince the basil leaves and add to the bowl along with the green onions. Toss with the vinaigrette. Best served at room temperature. Makes 4 servings.

2   teaspoons olive oil

3   green onions, chopped

1   teaspoon garlic

8   ounces imitation crab, flaked

1   cup dried breadcrumbs, divided (you need 6 slices of dried bread for 1 cup of breadcrumbs)

1   tablespoon lemon juice

1   egg

2   tablespoons mayonnaise

2   teaspoons Dijon mustard

2   teaspoons Worcestershire sauce

1   tablespoon freshly chopped dill weed or parsley

Crab Cakes

I've had crab cakes in many different parts of the country, and everyone seems to have their own regional spin on the flavors. The ingredient that keeps the crab cakes together (besides egg) is some sort of breadcrumbs or cracker crumbs. In this case, your stale bread comes in very handy. I let the bread dry out for several days at room temperature, and then make dried crumbs using a food processor or blender. Try this with rye bread crumbs sometime—yum!

In a small sauté pan heat the olive oil and brown the green onions and garlic; cool. Place the crab in a food processor and process until finely chopped. Add ¾ cup breadcrumbs, the lemon juice, egg, mayonnaise, mustard, Worcestershire, dill weed or parsley, and the onion-garlic mixture. Process until well blended and all ingredients are distributed. Remove from the food processor and shape into 6 to 8 crab cakes, depending on size desired. Dredge each crab cake in the remaining breadcrumbs. Brown in a little olive oil over medium high heat for 3 minutes on each side. Finish cooking by microwaving for 2 minutes on medium, or bake covered at 350° for 15 minutes. Makes 6 to 8 crab cakes.

Georgia Bread Pudding

There are hundreds of variations of bread pudding; it is a very versatile recipe. It's possible to incorporate any number of flavors and add all types of fruit or nuts in various combinations. I accumulate slices of leftover bread in a big open paper bag at room temperature, so that the bread dries out. When the bag looks full, I make this recipe.

2 tablespoons butter
½ loaf dried bread
¼ cup sugar
½ teaspoon cinnamon
1 egg
1 15-ounce can sliced peaches with juice
2 tablespoons Amaretto liqueur or Southern Comfort
½ cup milk
½ cup pecans

Preheat the oven to 375°. Place the butter in an 8 x 10-inch glass baking dish and place in the oven. In a very large mixing bowl break up the dried bread slices with your hands into cubes, or slice with a knife. Add the sugar and cinnamon and stir to distribute. In a small bowl beat the egg slightly and then add it to the large bowl along with the peaches and their juice, the liqueur, and the milk. Stir for about 5 minutes until the bread cubes are evenly coated. Stir in the pecans to distribute. Remove the baking pan from the oven, and pour the mixture into the pan. It will sizzle when it hits the pan. Level off the mixture with a spatula. Bake for 40 minutes. Makes 8 to 10 servings.

¼   cup blanched almonds
½   loaf bread, each slice
    cut into 3 sticks
4   eggs
1   cup apple juice
1   teaspoon almond
    extract
1   tablespoon Amaretto
    liqueur
2   teaspoons sugar
2   or more tablespoons
    butter to fry the toast

Apple-Almond French Toast Sticks

*I've always loved French toast, but it can sometimes taste
bland. Rather than relying on the maple syrup poured over the
top, you can make the toast batter a little sweeter and more flavorful. The flavors of apple and almond taste wonderful together, and cutting the toast into sticks is a fun way to serve an
otherwise ordinary dish.*

On a baking sheet toast the almonds for 5 minutes in a
350° oven. Let cool, then chop very finely or process in a
food processor until they are coarse crumbs. In a 9 x 13-
inch pan, place the sticks of bread. In a large mixing bowl
beat the eggs. Add the apple juice, almond extract, liqueur,
and sugar. Mix thoroughly. Add the chopped almonds and
mix again. Pour over the bread sticks in the pan and allow
the bread to soak up the mixture. Heat the skillet or griddle to medium high heat. Add the butter and brown the
French toast for 3 minutes per side. You can transfer the
cooked pieces to a platter and keep them warm in the oven
until all are cooked. Makes 6 to 8 servings.

Also uses eggs

Savory Stuffed Pork Chops

Back in the days when you'd go to the butcher to buy your meat and poultry (before there were mega-supermarkets), you could have the butcher cut extra-thick pork chops for stuffing and roasting. They are a little harder to find these days, but some supermarkets do have thicker cuts. When you find them, make this recipe!

4	slices stale bread (try rye bread)
2	teaspoons olive oil
¼	cup chopped onion
1	stalk celery, chopped
¼	teaspoon dill weed
¼	teaspoon caraway seed
1	egg, beaten
2	cups chicken broth
	Paprika
4	thick pork chops, bone-in

Preheat the oven to 375°. To make the stuffing, cut the bread slices into small cubes and place in a large mixing bowl. In a small saucepan heat the olive oil and brown the onion and celery until golden. Sprinkle with the dill and caraway, and stir to bring out the flavors. Add to the bread cubes. Stir in the egg. Add one cup of broth and stir to moisten. Add additional broth until the mixture is evenly wet and sticks together.

Make a horizontal slice in each pork chop, cutting through until you hit the bone. Stuff the bread mixture into the pork chops. Sprinkle the pork chops with paprika. In the same skillet you used to brown the onion, heat a little olive oil and brown the pork chops on each side for 2 minutes. Transfer to a casserole dish. Pour the remaining broth in the bottom of the pan. Cover and bake for 45 minutes. Makes 4 hefty servings.

Just as you don't eat bread plain without anything on it or around it, you need to use up stale bread by adding things to it or around it. You will also need to add some kind of liquid to the recipe, not only to flavor the bread, but also to get it to bind to the other ingredients. Flavors that go well with bread can be savory, such as onion, celery, and herbs, especially when used with meat, fish, or poultry. Adding fruits and sweet liquids to bread will enhance its flavor as well. It's good to add some crunchy ingredient to the bread because it tends to be very soft when liquid is added to it, and the crunch is good for contrast. When using stale bread, make sure that there is no visible mold on it. Even bread that has been kept in the refrigerator may have mold on it, and you don't want a moldy taste in the new dish that you make!

NOTES

_____

_____

_____

_____

_____

_____

_____

_____

_____

_____

From the kitchen of —————

From the kitchen of —————

4
Buttermilk

Thicker than milk, but not as thick as sour cream, buttermilk is somewhere in between the two as a baking ingredient. Buttermilk is most often packaged in a one-pint or one-quart carton. That means when you've used the ½ cup or 1 cup of buttermilk to make shortcake or pancakes, there's always the rest of the carton taking up space in the refrigerator. And, as with all dairy products, it's best to use them up by the expiration date. The recipes in this chapter capitalize on the texture and thickening power of buttermilk as well as its own unique tartness.

Picnic Corn Bread

The tartness of buttermilk enhances the sweetness of corn in this unique cornbread recipe. Take some along on your next picnic or serve it warm out of the oven with honey.

Preheat the oven to 375°. Brush an 8-inch square pan with olive oil or spray with cooking spray. In a large bowl mix together the flour, sugar, baking powder, soda, salt, and cornmeal. In a food processor or blender place the melted butter and onion. Process until liquefied, then add the buttermilk and eggs and blend until smooth. Pour over the dry ingredients. Stir until no lumps remain, then add the sweet corn and stir until evenly distributed. Bake for 35 minutes. Makes 9 to 12 servings.

1 cup all-purpose flour
3 tablespoons sugar
2½ teaspoons baking powder
½ teaspoon baking soda
½ teaspoon salt
1 cup yellow cornmeal
¼ cup melted butter
½ cup diced onion
1½ cups buttermilk
2 eggs
2 ears sweet corn, kernels cut off cob

½ cup buttermilk
½ cup mayonnaise
¼ teaspoon onion powder
¼ teaspoon garlic powder
¼ teaspoon dried tarragon
¼ teaspoon dried basil
¼ teaspoon dill weed
½ teaspoon sugar

Lazy R Salad Dressing

It's fast and easy to make your own ranch dressing, adding in the herbs you like best. Because buttermilk is so inexpensive compared to bottled ranch dressing, it's also more economical.

In a blender or food processor combine all of the ingredients. Process until thoroughly mixed. Transfer to a bottle or jar with a lid and store in the refrigerator. Makes 1 cup.

Mississippi Catfish

Oven-frying fish that is high in natural oil is the perfect way to balance healthy cooking techniques with flavor. Buttermilk's stickiness keeps the breading on the fish and gives it a wonderful taste.

½ cup cornmeal
½ teaspoon paprika
½ teaspoon oregano
⅛ teaspoon cayenne
½ cup buttermilk
1 pound fresh catfish fillets
Olive oil

Preheat the oven to 400°. Line a 10 x 15-inch baking pan or cookie sheet with aluminum foil and spray the foil with cooking spray. On a paper plate mix together the cornmeal, paprika, oregano, and cayenne. Stir with a fork until well blended. Pour the buttermilk into a shallow bowl. Cut the catfish fillets into portion-sized pieces. Dip each piece in the buttermilk and then in the cornmeal mixture, making sure to dip both sides of each piece. Place on baking sheet. Drizzle olive oil over the fillets or spray with olive oil–flavored cooking spray. Bake for 25 minutes. Makes 4 servings.

2 cups whole wheat flour
2 cups all-purpose flour
2 tablespoons baking powder
⅓ cup brown sugar
½ cup butter
1¼ cups buttermilk
1 teaspoon vanilla
½ cup dried currants, raisins, or any diced dried fruit
½ cup chopped walnuts

Yorkshire Scones

I adapted a scone recipe to taste like those in the bakeries of northern England. Traditional scones may be made with milk or cream, but buttermilk lightens them up and is a wonderful contrast with whatever fruits or nuts you add.

Preheat the oven to 400°. Grease two 8-inch round cake pans or coat with cooking spray. In a large bowl blend the whole wheat flour, flour, baking powder, and brown sugar thoroughly. Cut the butter into pieces and add to the bowl. Mix, using an electric mixer, until fine crumbs form. Stir in the buttermilk and vanilla. Mix until well blended, then add the dried fruit and nuts and stir until distributed. Divide the dough into two pieces. Roll out each piece into a circle on a floured board. Transfer to the prepared pans. With a sharp knife, cut the surface of the dough slightly to mark 6 or 8 pie wedges. Bake for 15 minutes. These freeze very well. Makes 12 to 16 scones.

Open Sesame Biscuits

There are thousands of recipes for biscuits, and buttermilk creates a wonderful soft-textured biscuit. This recipe is a little unusual, with the addition of sesame seeds. Their oil adds a bit more moisture to the biscuit, resulting in a slightly richer taste. Serve these with marmalade or a tart jam.

¼	cup sesame seeds
2	cups all-purpose flour
2	teaspoons baking powder
½	teaspoon salt
½	teaspoon baking soda
½	cup butter
2	tablespoons honey
1	cup buttermilk

On a baking sheet toast the sesame seeds for 10 minutes in a 350° oven, then set aside. Increase the oven temperature to 400°. Line a cookie sheet or jellyroll pan with aluminum foil. In a large mixing bowl blend the flour, baking powder, salt, and baking soda. Add the butter and mix until crumbly. Add the honey and buttermilk and stir together until well blended. Stir in the sesame seeds. Turn out the dough onto a floured board. Roll out to 1-inch thickness. Cut with a biscuit cutter and place on the prepared baking sheet. Bake for 10 minutes or until lightly browned. Makes 12 biscuits.

Buttermilk is very tart and sour, so you'll want to choose contrasting flavors that provide sweetness, such as corn, sugar, honey, or fruit. Adding buttermilk to baked goods such as cakes and quick breads will yield more moisture and a heavier, coarser crumb consistency. Therefore, buttermilk is a good ingredient for increasing the richness or wetness of the final product. Its natural texture is smooth and sticky, making it an excellent choice for coating foods such as salad greens, vegetables, or fish.

NOTES

_____

_____

_____

_____

_____

_____

_____

_____

_____

_____

_____

_____

_____

_____

_____

From the kitchen of —————

From the kitchen of —————

5
Carrots

Are there wilty-looking carrots in your refrigerator's crisper? It may be time to cook them or use them in another dish. Even if carrots are a little limp, they maintain their flavor and are excellent in cooked dishes. Baby carrots are very popular these days; they are actually cut and shaped from larger carrots and then packaged in bags (and I naively thought they were grown that way!) Because the baby carrots don't have the protective peel, they can either dry out or get a little slimy if there's too much moisture in the package. They generally don't keep as long as whole carrots. So, no matter what size or shape of carrots you have, here are some great ways to use them up. If you are using baby carrots in these recipes, one whole carrot equals about 4 baby carrots.

Seeded Carrots

I originally used butter for this recipe and sautéed the seeds before adding the carrots. Today, I use olive oil instead, and roast the carrots in the oven for a crispier finish. This is a fun dish; the seeds stick to the carrots and they look very festive—like little orange porcupines.

2	cups baby carrots or carrot chunks
1	tablespoon sesame seed
1	teaspoon poppy seed
½	teaspoon celery seed
½	teaspoon onion powder
¼	teaspoon salt
⅛	teaspoon paprika
2	tablespoons olive oil

Preheat the oven to 400°. In a saucepan with a steamer basket steam the carrots for 15 minutes. In a mixing bowl combine the sesame seeds, poppy seeds, celery seeds, onion powder, salt, and paprika. Toss the carrots with the seed/spice mixture and olive oil. Bake for 20 minutes, until the carrots are cooked through and the sesame seeds are golden brown. Makes 4 servings.

1½ cups shredded carrots
1   cup broccoli flowerets,
    cut into small pieces
1   cup cooked rice
2   green onions, thinly
    sliced
1   egg
½   cup grated cheese
½   teaspoon paprika
½   teaspoon salt
¼   teaspoon thyme
¼   teaspoon dill weed

Confetti Carrot Bake

This is a versatile vegetable casserole; you can substitute other green vegetables for the broccoli, such as green beans or zucchini. Whatever you decide to use, keep it colorful. This dish keeps very well, and is a good choice for a potluck. Bake in a glass casserole for a pretty presentation.

Preheat the oven to 350°. In a saucepan with a steamer basket steam the carrots and broccoli together for 5 minutes. In a large mixing bowl mix together the rice, green onions, egg, cheese, paprika, salt, thyme, dill, and the cooked carrots and broccoli. Be sure to break up any lumps of rice so that the grains are separated. Transfer to a 1½-quart baking dish with a cover. Bake, covered, for 30 minutes.

Also uses cheese and rice

Pot of Gold

The vibrant orange color of carrots makes this a festive side dish to serve alongside meats or poultry. Rutabagas are normally used for this dish, but if you can't find them you can try turnips or parsnips instead.

2	large rutabagas, peeled and chopped
4	large carrots, cut into slices
1	teaspoon sugar
1	tablespoon butter
½	teaspoon salt

In a large saucepan place the rutabagas, carrots, and sugar; add enough water to cover. Cook over medium heat for about 25 minutes or until the carrots are cooked through. Remove from the heat. With a slotted spoon transfer the vegetables to a food processor or blender. Add the butter and salt, and purée the mixture. Taste it and add more salt if desired. Makes 4 to 6 servings.

1   cup butter

¾   cup sugar

2   eggs

1   teaspoon vanilla

1   cup mashed cooked
      carrots (about 4)

2   cups all-purpose flour

2   teaspoons baking
      powder

½   teaspoon salt

½   cup coconut

Buttercream frosting:

1½ cups confectioners'
      sugar

2   tablespoons butter

2   teaspoons grated
      orange rind

1   to 2 tablespoons
      orange juice or water

Golden Carrot Cookies

This is a wonderful soft cookie, delicious with a little butter-cream frosting on top. The carrots give these cookies a rich golden color, and add richness and body to the cookie dough.

Preheat the oven to 400°. Grease a cookie sheet. In a large mixing bowl cream the butter and sugar. Add the eggs, vanilla, and carrots, and mix thoroughly. Add the flour, baking powder, and salt, and blend again. Stir in the co-conut. Drop the dough by tablespoonfuls onto the pre-pared cookie sheet. Bake for 8 to 10 minutes; these brown very quicklym so keep an eye on them.

To make the frosting, in a medium bowl blend the confectioners' sugar with the butter; stir in the rind and juice until smooth. Spread on the cooled cookies. Makes 2 dozen.

Asian Chicken Soup

This quick soup has lots of wonderful flavors and Asian vegetables. Carrots play a supporting role to the Asian vegetables in this soup, but contribute some sweetness and some contrast in color.

In a large soup pot place the chicken, ginger chunk, onions, and carrots. Add the chicken broth and water. Bring to a boil and then lower the heat and simmer for 15 minutes. Remove the chicken breasts and set aside to cool. Add the snow peas, cabbage, and mushrooms to the pot and simmer for 10 minutes. Meanwhile, remove the chicken from the bones and chop into small chunks. Return the chicken to the soup; remove the ginger. Add 1 tablespoon of soy sauce, stir well, and taste. If desired add the other tablespoon of soy sauce. Makes 6 to 10 servings.

4   chicken breast halves, skin removed

1   1-inch chunk fresh ginger

6   green onions, cut into 1-inch pieces

4   carrots, cut into ½-inch slices

1   quart chicken broth

1   quart water

8   ounces snow peas

1   small head Napa or Chinese cabbage, chopped

8   ounces mushrooms, sliced

1   to 2 tablespoons soy sauce

Like many root vegetables, carrots have natural sugar and a sweet flavor. Because of that, carrots make a great addition to soups or other vegetable dishes that have more pungent or tart vegetables in them; carrots balance out the flavor. Because carrots can be shredded or diced or even puréed when cooked, they can conform to the various sizes and shapes needed in various recipes. When puréed, they make a great thickener for soups, sauces, or baked goods, with the bonus of adding some sweetness. Shredded carrots add moisture to a dish, especially when baked with starches like rice—or even in dishes such as good old carrot cake. Shredded carrots can be used in quick breads and used with fruits such as apples, raisins, and apricots. Diced or sliced carrots make a nice addition to almost any type of soup and add some color.

For more recipes that use up carrots, see:

Mango Crispy Salad, p. 46
Roasted Vegetable Chicken Soup, p. 62
Oven-Roasted Winter Vegetables, p. 117
Onion-Smothered Pot Roast, p. 118

NOTES

From the kitchen of —————

From the kitchen of —————

6
Celery

Celery does last quite a while in the refrigerator because it is usually packaged as a bunch. However, because it is so high in water content, it can dry out in the refrigerator or turn brown. Celery also loses its crispness fairly quickly, especially after the outer stalks are taken off the bunch. Sometimes the innermost, pale stalks and leaves are bitter and can only be used for soup. So when you go to your crisper to retrieve some celery for these recipes, the best thing to do is to clean up the entire bunch. Cut off the bruised or brown ends. Cut stalks off the bunch and toss away the hard base. Cut off the celery leaves and put them in a small plastic bag for soup. Trim away all bruises, wash all the stalks worth keeping, and put them in a fresh bag. Then you'll be one step ahead in terms of using up that celery. These recipes make use of celery's crispness and mild flavor.

Brown Rice Pilaf

Traditional pilaf is made in a saucepan on top of the stove. This oven version is much easier, and the slow cooking makes the brown rice very tender. Celery makes the rice taste just a little sweeter as well as adding additional moisture to the dish.

½ to 1 cup diced celery

½ cup diced onion

1 cup uncooked brown rice or brown basmati rice

2 cups chicken broth

Preheat the oven to 375°. Spray a 2-quart casserole dish with cooking spray, or brush it with olive oil. Place the celery and onion in the casserole, then add the rice. Add the broth, and stir until the ingredients are evenly distributed. Cover and bake for 1 hour. Makes 4 to 6 servings.

2	tablespoons slivered almonds
2	teaspoons olive oil
1	teaspoon minced garlic
2	large or 4 small stalks celery, strings removed and sliced on the diagonal
5	small zucchini, sliced on the diagonal
¼	teaspoon dried basil
¼	teaspoon dried thyme or 4 fresh thyme sprigs
¼	cup chicken broth
1	tablespoon capers

Zucchini-Celery Almandine

The crunch of celery is a wonderful addition to any dish, but when it's cooked it also adds sweetness to the dish. This vegetable sauté is a refreshing mixture with the additional crunch of almonds on top.

On a baking sheet toast the almonds in a 350° oven for 8 minutes; remove and set aside. In a covered skillet heat the olive oil and sauté the garlic for one minute. Add the celery and zucchini and sauté briefly. Sprinkle the basil and thyme on top and stir. Cover and cook over medium high heat for 10 minutes. Add the broth and capers and reduce the heat to low; cook, covered, for 5 more minutes. Remove the thyme sprigs if used. Sprinkle the almonds over the top and serve. Makes 4 to 6 servings.

Primavera Soup

This colorful soup is smooth and crunchy at the same time.
Although it appears to be a cream soup, it is somewhat deceiv-
ing; there is no cream in it! Instead, cauliflower provides a
purée base for the soup, making it low-calorie as well. This is
great as an appetizer soup.

1	head cauliflower
1	quart chicken broth
1	small onion, quartered
½	teaspoon liquid smoke flavoring
2	teaspoons butter
1	cup celery, julienned
½	cup green beans, julienned
½	cup shredded carrots
½	teaspoon dill weed
½	teaspoon salt

In a soup pot cook the cauliflower with the broth, onion, and flavoring for 20 minutes. With a slotted spoon remove the cauliflower and onion and purée in a blender or food processor, then set aside. In a skillet heat the butter and sauté the celery, green beans, carrots, and dill weed for 3 minutes until soft, then add to the soup pot. Cover and cook for 10 minutes. Return the puréed cauliflower to the soup pot. Add ½ cup or more of water to thin the soup to the preferred consistency. Add the salt. Heat through for about 5 more minutes and serve. Makes 6 servings.

1   cup shredded carrot
1   cup jicama, cut into
    matchsticks
4   stalks celery, cut into
    matchsticks
1   green onion, finely
    chopped
4   sprigs fresh cilantro,
    minced
½   mango
1   tablespoon juice from a
    fresh lime
    Peel from 1 lime

Mango Crispy Salad

Mango forms the base of a creamy dressing for the crispy veg-etables in this salad. The crunch of celery and jicama go well to-gether. If you can't find jicama in your supermarket, substitute one can of water chestnuts cut into matchsticks.

In a bowl mix the carrot, jicama, celery, onion, and cilantro together. In a blender purée the mango, lime juice, and lime peel. Pour over the vegetables and toss. Refrigerate. Makes 4 to 6 servings.

Also uses carrots

Tuna Rotelli Salad

Pickle relish and celery have always been standard ingredients in my tuna salad. This recipe is a dressed-up version with pasta and other vegetables added. This is a nice, light, main-dish salad to serve for lunch.

In a large saucepan boil the pasta according to package directions; drain in a colander. In a large bowl mix together the celery, onions, cucumber, tomatoes, parsley, and tuna, then mix in the pasta. In a small bowl whisk together all of the ingredients for the dressing. Pour the dressing over the salad and mix in thoroughly. Serve immediately, or refrigerate. Makes 4 main-dish servings.

4	ounces Rotelli (cork-screw) pasta
¾	cup thinly sliced celery, cut on the diagonal
2	green onions, thinly sliced
½	cucumber, cut into matchsticks
8	cherry tomatoes, halved
1	tablespoon chopped parsley
1	6-ounce can tuna, drained

Dressing:

½	cup mayonnaise
1	tablespoon balsamic vinegar
1	teaspoon sugar
½	teaspoon onion powder
1	tablespoon water
½	teaspoon garlic
1	tablespoon sweet pickle relish

For more recipes that use up celery, see:

Roasted Vegetable Chicken Soup, p. 62

The key to working with celery is to maximize its crunchy texture and its slightly salty flavor. You'll want to add it to dishes that provide a contrasting texture, such as smooth or soft (like the soup or the mango salad). The salty flavor should be balanced with something that is sweet, such as onion, fruits of various types, sugar, or honey. When cooked, celery has a lot of water content that is released into the dish you are cooking, so when added to a starchy dish like rice it will contribute additional cooking liquid. Finally, the light green color of celery makes it a great addition to salads, and it keeps its crunch when served cold or with any type of dressing on it. As a cooking staple, celery is almost as versatile as onions, and there are many different dishes you can create with it.

NOTES

From the kitchen of _____

From the kitchen of _____

7
Cheese

Chunk or grated cheese comes in a multitude of varieties today, but no matter what size of package, there always seems to be some left over. Every person is different when it comes to cheese: sharp or mild, aged or not, shredded or sliced or in a slab. There are Cheddar cheeses and Swiss varieties and mozzarella and Monterey Jack and Colby, and low-fat or no-fat versions of all those. Perhaps that's why the average family usually has some cheese that needs to be used up—no two people like the same kind! The types of cheese in this chapter are those that you can shred or slice or melt. There are many other types of cheeses, such as Brie and Camembert, feta, blue, and Stilton, that have totally different cooking properties, so they are not covered here.

Easy Cheesy Garlic Bread

Remember the days of making garlic bread when you bought a loaf of white French bread, mixed butter with garlic powder and spread it on top? That was the garlic bread of the sixties. Today, most supermarkets have a wide variety of crusty "country" breads that have a lot more flavor and character. And instead of butter, it has become more common to see olive oil used on bread, often served in restaurants next to the bread-basket. So, this is an updated, versatile recipe for garlic bread that also helps you use up your cheese.

In a small bowl combine the olive oil and minced garlic. Let sit for 1 hour at room temperature.

Preheat the broiler. On the rack of a broiler pan arrange the bread slices. Brush the bread with the olive oil–garlic mixture. In a small bowl mix together the oregano and basil and sprinkle on top. Grind some pepper on top of each slice. Sprinkle the mushrooms over each slice, then the cheese. Broil for 2 to 5 minutes or until the cheese melts. Serve immediately. Makes 6 servings.

1	tablespoon olive oil
½	teaspoon minced garlic
6	1-inch slices of crusty bread such as sourdough, French, or Italian
¼	teaspoon oregano
¼	teaspoon dried basil
	Cracked pepper from a peppermill
4	fresh mushrooms, finely diced
	Up to ½ cup grated cheese (mozzarella, Cheddar, or even Swiss)

1   teaspoon olive oil
1   cup sliced mushrooms
1   zucchini, sliced very thin
2   green onions, sliced thin
4   eggs
1   egg white
¼   teaspoon basil
½   teaspoon salt
    Cracked pepper
½   cup shredded
    mozzarella or other
    cheese

Mushroom-Zucchini Frittata

A frittata is an Italian omelet that is made partly on top of the stove and then finished in the oven. Unlike a quiche, a frittata does not have milk or cream in it; it is mostly eggs. This dish is as versatile as omelets are; you can add a great number of different vegetables or seasonings, and, yes, cheese.

Preheat the oven to 375°. In an ovenproof skillet or cast-iron pan heat the olive oil and brown the mushrooms, zucchini, and onions until golden brown. Remove from the heat. In a medium bowl beat together the eggs, egg white, basil, salt, and pepper. Sprinkle the cheese evenly over the vegetable mixture, then pour the egg mixture on top. Bake for 15 minutes. Makes 6 to 8 servings.

Also uses eggs

Italian Picnic Torta

This recipe is like a stuffed pizza, but it is meant to be served cold or at room temperature. It takes a little bit of time to put the layers together, but it is worth it. When it is cut into wedges, you can see the vivid colors of the filling layers. Portable, festive, and yummy!

Dough:

3 cups bread flour

1 teaspoon salt

1 tablespoon instant yeast

¼ cup olive oil

1 cup warm water at "bread" temperature (105°)

Filling:

2 teaspoons olive oil

1 teaspoon minced garlic

1 pound fresh spinach leaves

1 12-ounce jar roasted peppers

1 cup grated mozzarella cheese

8 ounces thinly sliced smoked turkey

To prepare the dough, in a large bowl mix together 2 cups flour, the salt, and yeast, and blend thoroughly. Add ¼ cup olive oil and blend again. Add the water and mix, adding enough additional flour to clean the sides of the bowl. Turn out onto a floured board and knead until smooth and elastic. Place in an oiled bowl, cover with a towel, and let rise in a warm place for 45 minutes. Preheat the oven to 450°. Spray a 12 x 15-inch deep-dish pizza pan with cooking spray. Divide the dough in half. On a floured board, roll out half of the dough into a circle big enough to cover the bottom of the pan and extend up the sides to the edge. If possible, leave a little dough hanging out over the edge to make it easier to seal the top later on.

In a skillet heat 2 teaspoons olive oil and sauté the garlic, then sauté the spinach in two batches, keeping the cooked spinach in separate bowls. Drain the roasted peppers and blot with paper towels. Cut into ½-inch-wide strips. Layer the ingredients in the crust as follows: half of the cheese, half of the spinach, half of the turkey, all of the roasted peppers, remaining turkey, remaining cheese, remaining spinach.

Roll out the remaining dough and fit it over the pan. Fold the edge of the top over the bottom crust and pinch to seal. Let rise for 15 minutes. Bake for 25 minutes on the middle rack. Remove from the oven and brush with olive oil. Allow to cool in pan, then remove to a plate or cutting board so that the bottom doesn't get too soggy. Cut into wedges. Makes 6 to 10 servings.

2   large Idaho baking
    potatoes
2   tablespoons cornstarch
¼   teaspoon salt
¼   teaspoon paprika
2   tablespoons finely
    chopped onion
1   cup grated cheese
1   cup chicken broth
1   tablespoon olive oil
¼   teaspoon dried parsley
    or chervil

Potato Gratin

Au gratin potatoes often have milk and cheese in them. This recipe uses chicken broth as the liquid instead of milk, resulting in a lighter version. This is a great side dish to serve with barbecued meat, fish, or poultry. You can double the recipe for a family-sized crowd.

Preheat the oven to 350°. Brush a 1½-quart casserole with olive oil. Slice the potatoes into very thin slices, leaving the skin on if you prefer. Layer half of the potatoes in the casserole. Sprinkle with half of the cornstarch, salt, and paprika. Then sprinkle with half of the onion and half of the cheese. Repeat the layers. In a small bowl mix together the broth and olive oil and pour over the potatoes. Sprinkle the parsley or chervil on top. Bake, covered, for 45 minutes. If you want the top more browned, uncover for the last 15 minutes of cooking time. Makes 4 servings.

Also uses potatoes

Breakfast Burritos

*This dish is a wonderful spicy change from routine breakfast
fare. The cheese, chilies, and onions make a luscious combination. I've served these for tailgate parties and brunch; they are
very portable as long as they can be reheated a little at the des-
tination.*

1	tablespoon olive oil
4	green onions, sliced thin
1	4-ounce can diced chilies
6	eggs
½	teaspoon salt
1	avocado, cut into cubes
8	flour or corn tortillas
1	cup grated cheese

Preheat the oven to 350°. Brush a 9 x 13-inch baking dish
with olive oil. In a large skillet heat the olive oil and
brown the onions; add the chilies and stir. In a medium
bowl beat the eggs with the salt, then pour into the pan.
Add the avocado cubes, and stir until the eggs are softly
scrambled. Remove from the heat. Spray each tortilla with
a little water from a spray bottle to keep it from drying
out. Spoon some egg filling into each tortilla, then sprinkle with cheese. Roll up the tortillas and place in the prepared baking pan. Cover the baking pan with foil and
bake for 20 minutes. Makes 4 to 8 servings.

Also uses eggs

When it comes to cooking with cheese, the most important property it has is the ability to melt and stick to other things. That's why it's used in layered dishes such as lasagne or potatoes or any type of hot or grilled sandwich. One way to start thinking about cheese is what you want it to stick to; it might be vegetables, meats or poultry, rice or grains, breads, or eggs. The other key element is flavor. Because cheese is a fermented product, it has a tangy taste, making it an excellent choice to use with ingredients that are somewhat bland or even slightly sweet. Another aspect of cheese is texture. When melted and still hot, it is smooth and creamy. When it cools, it can become rubbery. If you're putting it in a dish that will be cooled somewhat before it's served, will the texture be objectionable in the dish? The last consideration is the volume; a little bit of grated or sliced cheese goes a long way. Think of it as concentrated flavor. Even when used to stick things together, it takes just a little bit of cheese.

2 fer For more recipes that use up cheese, see:

Confetti Carrot Bake, p. 36
Rainbow Lasagne, p. 60
Inside-Out Breakfast, p. 67

NOTES

_____

_____

_____

_____

_____

_____

_____

From the kitchen of ⸺

From the kitchen of ⸺

8
Chicken (Rotisserie)

I just love barbecued chicken of any kind, and when my local supermarkets started selling rotisserie chickens in the deli section, I bought them every week. Then, the novelty wore off. Soon, I had one-third or one-half of the chicken still on the carcass, waiting for my creative license. So, I rolled up my sleeves, took all the meat off the bones, and got to work. The average rotisserie chicken is enough to feed a family of four for one meal, but there actually is a lot more there than just four servings, so don't throw away the rest. The unique barbecued flavor of the chicken is a delightful addition to a number of new dishes.

Chinese Chicken Salad

There are dozens of different ways to make Chinese chicken salad. Using rotisserie chicken gives the salad more of a freshly grilled flavor, contrasting with the tart dressing and crunchy lettuce. You can expand the recipe for as many people as you need to serve, and can vary the amount of chicken depending on how much you have to use up.

In a large mixing bowl toss the lettuce, cucumber, celery, and onion. In a sauté pan heat the sesame oil over medium high heat and sauté the ginger and garlic until lightly browned. Add the chicken and cook for 2 minutes until the chicken is hot. Add the rice vinegar to the pan, and stir. Pour over the lettuce mixture in the bowl and stir to coat. Serve immediately.

For each serving:

1 cup shredded or coarsely cut crisp lettuce such as romaine

½ cucumber, peeled, seeded, and sliced into matchsticks

½ stalk celery, sliced very thin

1 green onion, sliced thinly on diagonal

1 teaspoon toasted sesame oil

1 thumb-sized piece fresh ginger, minced

1 clove garlic, minced

½ to ¾ cup rotisserie chicken bits and pieces

1 tablespoon rice vinegar

1   whole eggplant
1   to 1½ cups rotisserie
    chicken bits
1   cup chard leaves or
    spinach
2   teaspoons olive oil
½   cup sliced mushrooms
1   16-ounce container
    low-fat ricotta cheese
½   teaspoon chopped
    garlic
½   teaspoon dried basil
1   egg
1   8-ounce package
    regular lasagne noodles
1   26-ounce jar pasta
    sauce (marinara or
    tomato basil works
    best)
1   cup grated mozzarella
    cheese

Rainbow Lasagne

*Chicken bits blended with roasted eggplant create a pâté layer
for this colorful lasagne. The tomato sauce and spinach add red
and green to complete the rainbow. Lasagna takes a while to
put together because of all the layers, but once it's made it goes
a long way. This is a robust and filling lasagna. It also freezes
well.*

Cut the eggplant in half, and brush lightly with olive oil.
Roast in a 400° oven for about 20 minutes or until soft.
Allow to cool. With a spoon, remove the pulp. Place in a
blender or food processor with the chicken bits and
process. The mixture should resemble pâté. Set aside.
Reduce the oven temperature to 375°. Slice the chard
leaves. In a skillet heat the olive oil and sauté the chard
leaves with the mushrooms until the chard is wilted and
the mushrooms are lightly browned. Set aside. In a mixing
bowl blend the ricotta cheese with the garlic, basil, and
egg. Cook the lasagne noodles according to package directions. Drain.

Lightly brush a 9 x 13-inch baking pan with olive oil.
Place layers in the pan as follows: one-third of the tomato
sauce; one-third of the lasagne noodles; all of the ricotta
mixture; all of the chard-mushroom mixture; one-third of
the grated mozzarella; one-third of the lasagne noodles;
one-third of the sauce; all of the chicken-eggplant mixture; one-third of the mozzarella; remaining lasagne noodles; remaining sauce; remaining mozzarella. Cover the
pan with aluminum foil and bake for 45 minutes. Makes
8 to 12 servings.

2 *fer*

Also uses cheese

Chicken-Artichoke Pasta

This pasta sauce is fast and easy, and the chicken gives it a wonderful grilled flavor. Use the sauce on a long pasta such as spaghetti or linguine.

1	tablespoon olive oil
1	cup sliced mushrooms
1	teaspoon minced garlic
1	cup artichoke hearts
¼	teaspoon dried basil
¼	teaspoon oregano
1	tablespoon all-purpose flour
¾	cup chicken broth
¼	cup white wine
	Up to 1 cup shredded or diced chicken

In a large skillet heat the olive oil and brown the mushrooms and garlic for 2 minutes, until the mushrooms release their moisture. Add the artichoke hearts and sauté for 2 more minutes. Sprinkle the basil, oregano, and flour over the mixture, then add the broth and wine. Add the chicken, and reduce the heat to medium. Cook for about 5 minutes, until the sauce thickens. Serve over hot cooked pasta of your choice. Makes 4 servings.

1   cup baby carrots, cut crosswise into thirds

1   cup celery, cut into ½-inch pieces

1   onion, chopped into 1-inch pieces

½   teaspoon basil

1   tablespoon olive oil

3   ounces fettuccine, broken into 2-inch pieces

1   quart chicken broth

1   cup or more chopped chicken

2   tablespoons chopped parsley

1   cup water
    Salt and pepper to taste

Roasted Vegetable Chicken Soup

Mother's chicken soup was never like this. Roasting the traditional chicken soup vegetables first adds more of a smoky taste, which complements the flavor of the chicken. This fast but elegant recipe makes a very flavorful soup in just an hour.

Preheat the oven to 425°. In a flat, foil-lined baking pan, place the carrots, celery, and onion. Sprinkle with basil and olive oil and toss to coat. Roast for 30 minutes. Meanwhile, cook the fettuccine according to package directions and drain.

In a soup pot heat the chicken broth. Add the roasted vegetables and chicken, then add the parsley. Simmer for 15 minutes. Add the water and fettuccine, and heat through for 5 minutes more. Add salt and pepper to taste. Makes 6 servings.

Also uses carrots and celery

Brown Rice Jambalaya

Jambalaya is a wonderful mixture of vegetables, meats, and seasonings. Using brown rice gives it a nutty flavor, and using rotisserie chicken makes it even better. This is a hearty one-dish meal.

1	tablespoon olive oil
1	cup chopped onion
½	cup diced celery
½	cup diced green pepper
1	teaspoon minced garlic
2½	cups chicken broth
½	teaspoon salt
⅛	teaspoon cayenne
1	cup brown rice
1	cup or more chopped chicken
2	zucchini, cut into ½-inch slices
1	smoked chicken sausage sliced (optional)

In a Dutch oven or large covered braising pan heat the olive oil and brown the onion, celery, green pepper, and garlic for about 5 minutes. Add the broth, salt, and cayenne. Add the rice, cover, reduce the heat, and simmer for 30 minutes. Add the chicken, zucchini, and sausage. Cover and simmer for 30 more minutes, or until the rice is cooked through. Makes 4 to 6 servings.

Also uses onions

The main thing to keep in mind for rotisserie chicken is that it is already cooked, so you don't want to overcook it or it will become tough. You want to cook it long enough to flavor the dish, but that's all. Because you have to take the chicken off the carcass, you will always have small chunks and pieces of chicken. Therefore, you should always make dishes that are going to work with small pieces of chicken. Rice dishes, soups, pastas, and salads work well. You can also grind the chicken and blend it with other things, as in the lasagne recipe in this chapter. As far as flavor, the chicken has some inherent flavor already, and some chickens might be cooked with barbecue sauce, spicy sauce, or lemon and herbs. Adding this chicken to other dishes means that you probably won't want to add a lot of other new seasonings or it might just be too much. The best way to approach it is to add a very small amount of other spices and herbs, and then go by taste.

NOTES

From the kitchen of _____

From the kitchen of _____

9
Eggs

As the commercial goes, the "incredible, edible egg." Such versatility and fragility in just one food. Recently bashed by cholesterol-fearing eaters, eggs are once again redeeming themselves. Now you can find lower-cholesterol eggs, organic eggs, cage-free eggs, and eggs with additional nutrients. Whatever the type, eggs are still packaged for the most part by the dozen. Sometimes you can find half-cartons, but not always. So, if you don't cook a lot of eggs to eat just plain for breakfast, you will have some left. For safety it is recommended that you keep fresh eggs in the refrigerator no longer than a week (Appendix). That's only seven days, and in a two-person household, that's a lot of eggs to use up in a very short time. So, it's off to find some recipes to use up eggs!

Inside-Out Breakfast

Breakfast sandwiches made of ham, eggs, and cheese on a bun or English muffin have become a staple at fast-food restaurants and in the freezer section at the grocery store. It's healthier to make your own—not to mention more economical—but making individual breakfast sandwiches at home can be time-consuming. This dish is a variation on the breakfast sandwich, except that the eggs are on the outside, not the inside—hence the name. They also freeze well and are a great way to use up eggs. You can make a lower-calorie version of this by using turkey ham and thin-sliced bread. You can also substitute soy milk or rice milk for regular milk.

8	slices bread
4	thin slices deli ham or turkey ham
1	cup grated cheese
8	eggs
1	cup milk
½	teaspoon salt
½	teaspoon paprika

Preheat the oven to 350°. Toast the bread lightly. Spray a 9 x 13-inch pan with cooking spray and place 4 slices of toast on the bottom of the pan. Place 1 slice of ham on each slice of bread. Sprinkle half of the grated cheese on top of the ham. Place the other slices of toast on top. Now you have four "sandwiches." Take a knife and cut each sandwich in quarters (this will allow the egg mixture to soak into the center). In a medium bowl beat together the eggs, milk, salt, and paprika. Pour over the sandwiches, being careful not to disturb the stacks. Sprinkle with the remaining cheese and a bit more paprika. Let sit at room temperature for 10 minutes. Bake, covered, for 40 minutes. Makes 4 to 6 servings.

Also uses cheese and milk

1   cup butter, melted

2¾ cups sugar

5   eggs

1   teaspoon vanilla

3   cups all-purpose flour

1   teaspoon baking
     powder

½   teaspoon salt

1   8-ounce can crushed
     pineapple (reserve juice)

¼   cup rum

Glaze:

½   cup sugar

¼   cup reserved pineapple
     juice

2   tablespoons rum

Paradise Pound Cake

Pound cake is a great way to use up eggs. This unusual version combines the flavors of pineapple and rum for a tropical taste. Baking it in a 10-inch tube pan makes for a beautiful presentation as well. Elegant enough for a dinner party, yet portable enough to take to a picnic or potluck.

Preheat the oven to 350°. Spray a nonstick bundt or tube pan with cooking spray. In a large mixing bowl cream the butter and 2¾ cups sugar until smooth, then beat in the eggs and vanilla. In a medium bowl combine the flour, baking powder, and salt, and add to the mixture. Add the drained pineapple and rum, and blend until smooth. Turn into the prepared pan. Bake for 1 hour or until a toothpick inserted in the center comes out clean. Let cool for 5 minutes in the pan, then turn out onto a plate.

In a small saucepan cook ½ cup sugar and pineapple juice over medium high heat for 5 minutes, stirring constantly. Stir in 2 tablespoons rum. With a thin skewer or toothpick, poke holes all the way around the cake. Spoon the glaze over, distributing evenly and giving it time to soak into the cake. Makes 12 to 16 servings.

Everyday Noodles

My mother always made homemade noodles, especially for soup. For her, it was faster to stir up a bunch of noodles than it was to go to the store to buy them. Noodles (or "pasta" as we now call them) are a great way to use up eggs, and once you taste the homemade version, you will be spoiled! You don't need a pasta machine to shape noodles. Merely roll them out on a floured board and cut with a sharp knife. That's all there is to it.

3 eggs
½ teaspoon salt
1 tablespoon olive oil or melted butter
2 cups all-purpose flour

In a mixing bowl combine the eggs and salt, and beat well. Add the oil or butter, then the flour, and mix into a stiff dough. If it seems wet, add a little more flour until you can form the dough into a ball. Divide the dough in half. Cover one-half of the dough with a towel and keep in the refrigerator. Roll out the remaining dough as thin as you can; ⅛-inch thickness or paper-thin. Let dry on a board covered with a towel for about 30 minutes. Cut in ¼-inch strips with a sharp knife. Sprinkle the noodles with a little flour and then set them aside on a flat pan until you're ready to use them as pasta or in soup. Repeat with the other half of the dough. You can keep the noodles in the refrigerator or freeze them; just sprinkle them with a little rice flour and store in an airtight bag until you're ready to use them. Makes enough for 8 servings of pasta or 2 batches of soup.

3   eggs
⅔   cup sugar
1   cup corn syrup (light or
    dark)
⅓   cup melted butter
¼   teaspoon salt
1   cup pecan halves
    Prepared 9-inch pie
    crust

Pecan Pie

The first time I tasted this pie, it became an instant favorite. It's so easy to make, and the pecans float magically to the top of the pie. You can use your favorite single pie crust recipe for this, or use a ready-made packaged crust.

Preheat the oven to 375°. In a large mixing bowl beat the eggs, sugar, and corn syrup. Add the melted butter and salt; stir in the pecans. Pour the mixture into the prepared pie crust. Bake for 40 to 50 minutes. Makes 6 to 8 servings.

Walnut Biscotti

There are literally hundreds of different flavors of biscotti. These Italian cookies require a lot of eggs, so they're great for using them up. This is one of my favorite versions of biscotti. You can vary it by using pine nuts or almonds instead of walnuts if you like.

1   cup sugar
½   cup butter, melted
2   tablespoons Anisette or Amaretto liqueur
1   tablespoon water
1   teaspoon vanilla
3   eggs
3¼ cups all-purpose flour
2   teaspoons baking powder
1   cup chopped walnuts

In a large mixing bowl blend the sugar, butter, liqueur, water, and vanilla until smooth. Add the eggs and beat thoroughly. Add the flour and baking powder and blend thoroughly, then stir in the walnuts. Refrigerate the dough for at least 3 hours.

Preheat the oven to 375°. Line two large cookie sheets or jellyroll pans with parchment paper or aluminum foil (spray the foil with cooking spray). Wet your hands and shape the dough into 3 loaves, 1 inch high and about 3 to 4 inches wide. Place on one of the prepared cookie sheets and smooth the edges of the loaves at the sides so they thin at the edges (this will create a more rounded shape). Bake for 30 minutes. Remove from the oven and let cool. Reduce the oven temperature to 275°. When cool, cut the loaves into ½-inch crosswise slices. Place the slices cut-side down on the prepared foil-lined cookie sheets. Bake for 40 minutes or until dry. You can double the recipe and make enough to give as gifts, which is something I do for the holidays. These store very well at room temperature in cookie tins. Makes at least 3 dozen biscotti.

Eggs can be used in so many different ways in recipes that the variations are endless. The yolks and the whites have different cooking properties, and you can use them separately in different recipes or together in the same recipe. When used whole in baked goods, eggs add body and help "set" other ingredients into a more solid form. They also will add a little bit of a golden color to otherwise white ingredients, such as flour. Egg whites whipped separately and added to dishes will give the dish a lighter texture. Egg yolks used by themselves will give the dish a heavier and richer texture. As a break-fast food, eggs are very versatile, and can be combined with vegetables, fruits, meats, and seasonings to liven up their flavor. Eggs can also coat things such as bread, potatoes, or rice, and they help everything stick together.

2 fer

For more recipes that use up eggs, see:

Apple Walnut Cheesecake, p. 7
David's Pancakes, p. 15
Apple-Almond French Toast Sticks, p. 22
Mushroom-Zucchini Frittata, p. 52
Breakfast Burritos, p. 55
Oven Pancake, p. 103
Orange Chiffon, p. 125
Sun-Rice Eggs, p. 155

NOTES

From the kitchen of _____

From the kitchen of _____

10
Honey

Honey is a great alternative to sugar in a lot of recipes, as well as an ingredient in Grandma's old remedy for a cold: drinking honey and lemon in hot water. Honey is packaged in glass jars or squeeze bottles of all sizes. Honey is best kept at room temperature; otherwise it will solidify. Even at room temperature, honey will form crystals, and it must be heated in order to pour it or squeeze it from the container. Because honey is such a concentrated and powerful sweetener, a little goes a long way. For that reason, it seems that there's always that partial jar of honey on the shelf, often sticking to the shelf below because it's been there a while. Well, it's time to get that honey out and make some fabulous new recipes with it.

Baklava Twists

Combine the taste of baklava with cinnamon rolls and what do you get? These wonderful sweet breads, with a hint of lemon and the scent of cinnamon. Wonderful with coffee.

3½	cups (approximately) unbleached flour
1	tablespoon yeast
¾	teaspoon salt
½	teaspoon cinnamon
1	cup milk
½	cup water
¼	cup honey
2	tablespoons vegetable oil

Filling:

¾	cup finely chopped walnuts, divided
2	tablespoons sugar
2	teaspoons grated lemon peel
½	teaspoon cinnamon
2	tablespoons butter
2	tablespoons warm honey

In a large mixing bowl place 2½ cups flour. Add the yeast, salt, and ½ teaspoon cinnamon, and stir until blended. In a saucepan heat the milk and water to "bread" temperature (105°) and add to the flour mixture. Add the honey and vegetable oil, then add enough additional flour so that the dough leaves the side of the bowl. Transfer to a floured board and knead until smooth and elastic. Put the dough in an oiled bowl, cover with a towel, and let rise in a warm place for 40 minutes or until doubled.

To make the filling, set aside 2 tablespoons walnuts. In a small bowl mix the remaining walnuts with the sugar, lemon peel, and ½ teaspoon cinnamon. In a saucepan or the microwave melt the butter and honey together.

Preheat the oven to 375°. Line a cookie sheet with aluminum foil or parchment paper. Punch down the dough and roll out onto a floured board to a 21 x 8-inch rectangle. Brush the dough with half of the butter-honey mixture, then sprinkle the filling over the dough. Fold the dough into thirds, along the long side of the rectangle, so that you wind up with a log 8 inches long and 7 inches wide. Cut through the log to make 12 strips. Twist each strip once or twice and press down the ends so that it stays in a spiral. Transfer the strips to the prepared cookie sheet. Brush the twists with the rest of the butter-honey mixture and sprinkle with the reserved walnuts. Let rise for 20 minutes. Bake for 15 minutes on the middle rack. Makes 1 dozen large twists.

Also uses milk

1   teaspoon minced garlic
2   thumb-sized slices fresh
    ginger, minced
¼   cup honey
1   cup reduced-sodium soy
    sauce
½   cup water
8   chicken thighs, or 1½
    pounds flank steak

Terrific Teriyaki

I learned how to make teriyaki chicken and beef by taste. My Polynesian cooking teacher always told me to "start with the ingredients that take the least amount" because then you can always add more to your taste. Honey makes the sauce stick to the meat so that it absorbs all the teriyaki flavors. The proportions below are approximate, but you can try it once and adjust it for your own taste.

In a small mixing bowl blend together the garlic and ginger. Add the honey and soy sauce. Add the water. Whisk or stir very well, and while the mixture is still moving, dip your finger in and taste it. Is it sweet enough? If not, add another tablespoon of honey until you have the right balance. Is it too salty? Add a little more water. It's not a good idea to add more ginger or garlic, because both of those flavors become stronger as the meat marinates. When you have the marinade adjusted for your taste, pour it over the chicken or beef in a glass dish, and marinate it for at least 6 hours or overnight. Cook on a barbecue grill over direct heat and serve. Makes 6 to 8 servings.

Honey-Lime Fruit Salad

When I had my catering company, this was my standard fruit salad. Because there is no dairy or mayonnaise, this salad can be outdoors for an event and it won't spoil. It's also a very pretty salad when served in a clear glass bowl.

In a medium bowl whisk together the ingredients for the dressing. In a large serving bowl combine all of the fruit, and pour the dressing on top. Refrigerate for at least 2 hours before serving to blend the flavors. Stir once before serving. Makes 10 to 12 servings.

Dressing:

- 2 tablespoons sugar
- 1 tablespoon lemon juice
- ⅛ teaspoon paprika
- ⅛ teaspoon salt
  Juice and peel of 2 limes (4 tablespoons juice and 2 teaspoons peel)
- 3 tablespoons honey
- ⅓ cup light salad oil such as canola

Fruit:

- ½ cantaloupe cut into chunks
- ½ honeydew melon cut into chunks
- 1 cup green or red grapes
- 1 cup strawberries sliced in half
- 1 cup of any of the following: kiwi fruit, peeled and sliced; raspberries; blueberries; peaches; oranges; or apricots

(*Note:* Apples and bananas should not be used because they will turn brown and give the salad an unpleasant taste.)

Marinade:

2   tablespoons honey
2   tablespoons lemon juice
     Grated rind of one
     lemon
1   cup of apple juice
1   teaspoon rubbed sage
½   teaspoon dried thyme
½   teaspoon onion powder
¼   teaspoon white pepper
¼   teaspoon salt

8   fresh sage leaves
1   leek or 4 green onions,
     cut into slivers
2   whole Cornish hens,
     washed and split in half

Basting sauce:

2   tablespoons honey
1   tablespoon olive oil
½   teaspoon minced garlic
1   teaspoon lemon juice
2   teaspoons cornstarch
1   tablespoon cold water

Honey-Sage Cornish Hens

Cornish hens are a nice change from chicken, and they taste wonderful with pungent herbs such as sage or rosemary. Honey's stickiness makes a great basting sauce during roasting.

In a small bowl whisk together the ingredients for the marinade. Place the sage leaves and some of the slivers of leek or onion under the skin of the Cornish hens. Place the hens in a shallow glass pan. Pour the marinade over, and refrigerate for at least 3 hours.

Preheat the oven to 425°. Remove the hens from the marinade and place them on a rack skin side down in a large shallow roasting pan. Reserve ½ cup of the marinade and place in a large glass measuring cup. Pour the remaining marinade in the bottom of the pan and add the rest of the leeks. Add enough water to cover the bottom of the pan.

For the basting sauce, add 2 tablespoons honey, the olive oil, garlic, and 1 teaspoon lemon juice to the measuring cup. Whisk together, then microwave on medium for 1 minute. In a small bowl mix the cornstarch with the water until blended. Add to the measuring cup and microwave again for 2 or 3 more minutes until thick, stirring after each minute.

Brush the sauce over the hens, coating the bone side first, then turn them over skin side up and coat that side. Roast for 30 minutes, then baste again with more sauce. Reduce the oven temperature to 400° and roast for 15 more minutes or until done. Makes 4 servings.

Sesame Drumettes with Dipping Sauce

This was one of the most popular items on my catering menu. Drumettes are the leg portion of a chicken wing, and you can buy them packaged in the supermarket. They have a convenient "handle," making them a perfect appetizer for dipping. I would also serve sugar snap peas alongside, which are wonderful dipped in the sauce as well.

2   tablespoons sesame seeds
½   cup canola oil
2   tablespoons soy sauce
¼   cup sherry
2   tablespoons lemon juice
1   teaspoon garlic
2   tablespoons honey
2   pounds chicken drumettes

Dipping sauce:
½   cup sesame tahini
2   tablespoons honey
½   teaspoon grated fresh ginger
1   tablespoon soy sauce
1   tablespoon sesame oil
1   tablespoon rice vinegar
1   to 2 tablespoons apple or orange juice

In a skillet toast the sesame seeds for 5 minutes over medium high heat until brown. Set aside. In a medium bowl mix together the oil, soy sauce, sherry, lemon juice, garlic, and honey, and blend well. Stir in the sesame seeds. Place the drumettes in a shallow glass dish and pour the marinade over. Refrigerate for at least 1 hour.

Remove from the refrigerator and broil for 7 minutes on each side. Allow to cool. Makes about 24 drumettes, depending on size.

To make the dipping sauce, in a blender mix the tahini, honey, ginger, soy sauce, sesame oil, and rice vinegar. Process until smooth. Add enough apple or orange juice to thin it to dipping consistency, keeping in mind that it will thicken a lot when it is chilled. Makes 1 cup.

Remember that the reason you probably have honey left over is that it is so concentrated, so a little does go a long way. If you want to substitute honey for sugar in a recipe, you will want to use a little less honey. The flavor of honey is very intense, and if you use too much in a recipe it can be cloying and overpower the other ingredients. Citrus flavors, such as lemon, lime, and orange, create a nice balance with honey. Honey is naturally sticky, so it's great in sauces that are used when cooking or barbecuing various foods. It's often an ingredient in homemade barbecue sauce. Onions and garlic work well with a little honey when cooking poultry or meats to add some sweetness. Honey can be used to provide a little sweetness to raw or cooked fruits, especially those that are a little tart. In baked goods, honey is a great substitute for sugar in most yeast breads, especially those with whole-wheat flour in the recipe.

NOTES

_____

_____

_____

_____

_____

_____

_____

From the kitchen of

From the kitchen of

11
Jam/Jelly

Don't you just love getting those food baskets during the holidays, with yet another jar of jelly or jam to put on the pantry shelf? You can eat only so much toast with jam on it, a teaspoon at a time. I've often wondered why jam is packaged in such a large jar, because you use so little of it at a time. Once jam or jelly is opened, it must be refrigerated. If it's been in the refrigerator too long, it will crystallize or even form mold. If it's moldy, throw it out. If it has crystals, it can probably still be used in recipes. The idea of using up jam is to find recipes that require more than a teaspoon. Jam or jelly can be made from almost any fruit imaginable. The most common jam flavor is strawberry, but others include raspberry, blueberry, blackberry, currant, peach, apricot, and even pineapple. Whatever flavor you have, it can be used in other dishes to create something new.

Jamuffins

These delightful muffins have a juicy surprise in the middle: fruit jam. Just right for breakfast, with oatmeal in the batter, they provide a healthy alternative and are not overly sweet.

2   medium bananas
½   cup (1 stick) margarine or butter
½   cup brown sugar
⅓   cup milk
½   teaspoon vanilla
1   cup oatmeal (not quick oatmeal)
1½ cups all-purpose flour
1   tablespoon baking powder
½   teaspoon baking soda
½   teaspoon salt
1   teaspoon of jam for each muffin

Preheat the oven to 375°. Lightly grease the tins of a muffin pan or use paper muffin cups. In a food processor or blender place the bananas, margarine or butter, and brown sugar. Process until no lumps remain. Add the milk and vanilla and process for 1 minute. In a large mixing bowl blend the oatmeal, flour, baking powder, soda, and salt; stir until well blended. Pour the wet ingredients over the dry ingredients, and stir until no lumps remain. With a large spoon fill the muffin cups one-half full. With a small spoon place a teaspoon of jam in the center of each muffin cup. Spoon the rest of the batter over the jam, distributing equally among all the muffins. Bake for 22 minutes. Allow to cool on a wire rack. Makes 12 muffins.

Also uses bananas

2 eggs, separated
½ cup sugar
½ teaspoon vanilla
2 tablespoons milk
1 tablespoon water
½ cup cake flour
½ teaspoon baking
   powder
⅛ teaspoon salt
4 to 6 ounces leftover jam

Jam Cake Roll

Jam or jelly makes a natural and easy filling for a classic sponge cake roll. This recipe has been downsized to fit a 9 x 13-inch pan, which can accommodate up to ¾ cup of jam. Any flavor of jam will work, depending on your tastes. I've made this with peach and cherry jam, but raspberry, strawberry, and blackberry would work well also.

Preheat the oven to 375°. Spray a 9 x 13-inch baking pan with cooking spray or lightly brush with oil. In a large bowl beat the egg yolks with the sugar until lemon-colored. Add the vanilla, milk, and water, and beat until blended. Add the flour, baking powder, and salt, and blend until smooth. In a separate bowl beat the egg whites until stiff. Fold into the batter. Spread the batter into the pan, distributing it evenly with a spatula. Bake for 10 to 12 minutes on the middle rack.

Meanwhile, sprinkle a finely woven kitchen towel (not terrycloth) with powdered sugar. Remove the cake from the oven and invert it onto the prepared towel. Allow to cool for about 5 minutes. Spread the jam over the cake, then gently roll from either edge, depending on whether you want a thick roll with few slices, or a thin roll with more slices. Allow the cake to cool thoroughly. Cut into slices to serve. Makes about 12 servings.

BBQ Beef Ribs

I just love to roll up my sleeves and get all messy eating ribs. Pork ribs, especially baby-back ribs, are more common these days, and it's becoming more difficult to find beef ribs in restaurants. To make beef ribs tender, they need to be roasted first at a high temperature without sauce and then slow-roasted with sauce. The magic ingredient in this sauce? Jam, of course. It provides a sweet contrast with the tangy tomato, mustard, and chili flavors and gives the sauce the perfect consistency for sticking to the ribs. Prepare to get messy!

Place the ribs in a shallow glass pan or a large zippered plastic bag. In a small bowl mix together the ingredients for the marinade and pour over the ribs. Marinate in the refrigerator for 4 hours.

In a saucepan mix all of the ingredients for the sauce and bring to a simmer. Cook until the sauce is smooth and the jam melts, about 5 to 10 minutes.

Preheat the oven to 450°. Place the ribs on a rack in a shallow roasting pan. Roast for 15 minutes, then turn the ribs over and roast for 15 more minutes. Reduce the oven temperature to 350°, spoon on the sauce, and return to the oven for 45 minutes, basting with sauce every 15 minutes. Makes 4 to 6 servings.

2 pounds beef ribs

Marinade:

1 cup wine (red is better but white works too)

1 teaspoon oregano

1 teaspoon garlic

2 tablespoons olive oil

Sauce:

1 8-ounce can tomato sauce

½ cup red jam (berry flavor is best, such as strawberry or blackberry)

½ teaspoon onion powder

1 tablespoon prepared mustard

1 tablespoon Worcestershire sauce

½ teaspoon chili powder

1 tablespoon lemon juice

Also uses wine

8   slices French toast (your
     favorite recipe)
¼   cup peanut butter
¼   to ½ cup jam, any flavor

(*Note:* If you are allergic to
peanuts, you can use
almond butter instead.)

pBJ French Toast

*This recipe may sound a little weird, but reserve judgment until
you taste it. I ordered a dish similar to this in a restaurant once,
and it was delicious and filling. You don't need to use any syrup
on it, because the jam is already in it. And it goes without say-
ing that the kids will like it, too.*

While the French toast is still hot, spread each slice with 1
tablespoon of peanut butter and 1 or 2 tablespoons of
jam. Place a second slice of French toast on top to form a
sandwich. Cut on the diagonal and serve on a plate.
Makes 4 hearty servings.

Berriest Smoothie

Smoothies are all the rage these days. They're the milk shake of the twenty-first century. Because smoothies are supposed to be at least a little healthy, you don't want to add a lot of sugar to them. Adding jam is a great alternative, because it has fruit and just a little bit of sugar. This berry version is a really pretty color as well. The recipe is for one smoothie, so just multiply the recipe by the number of people you want to serve.

1   cup milk, any kind
1   tablespoon almond butter
½   cup fresh or frozen strawberries
¼   cup blueberries
¼   cup strawberry or raspberry sorbet
2   tablespoons berry jam (strawberry, blackberry, raspberry, blueberry)

In a blender combine all of the ingredients and purée until smooth. Serve in a tall glass. If it's too thick for your taste, add a little more milk.

Also uses milk

Jam is a very concentrated form of fruit and sugar. Therefore, it can be used as a sweetener in some foods without being overpowering. The fruit in jam lightens up the sweetness, and also adds additional flavor. Because there are so many different flavors of jam, choose a dish that might blend well with that particular fruit flavor. Jam can be used as a glaze for meats, poultry, or seafood, and its stickiness acts to keep the flavor on the food as it is cooked. Jam helps to thicken sauces or other ingredients as well. As any kid will tell you, jam complements nuts or nut butters very well. It can be used as a cake filling or as a cake or cookie topping. Use it in cooked fruit dishes, such as a baked cobbler or crisp, or on fresh fruits, with a little lemon or orange juice as a fruit salad dressing.

2 fer
For more recipes that use up jam or jelly, see:
Barbecue Pork Kebabs, p. 198

NOTES

From the kitchen of —————

From the kitchen of —————

12

Lemons

Pucker up, it's the lemon chapter! I love the smell of fresh lemons, and they are a colorful piece of décor in the kitchen as well. However, when your lemons go from shiny to dull and start looking a little withered, it's time to use them up. If you are lucky enough to have a lemon tree (or are close to a neighbor's lemon tree), then that's good news and bad news. The good news is, you have an endless supply of lemons just ready to pick for several months of the year. The bad news is, you have an endless supply of lemons, and they won't keep forever on that tree. So, whether you get them from your yard or from the store, you're bound to have a need to somehow use up those lemons. Lemons consist of two important parts used in cooking: the peel on the outside and the juice on the inside. These recipes use a little bit of both.

Lemon Tarragon Chicken Tenders

Most every supermarket has little strips of chicken breast called chicken tenders. You can even buy them frozen in large bags and just take out whatever you need. The lemon peel and juice make the chicken light and refreshing.

2	lemons
½	teaspoon dry tarragon
½	teaspoon onion powder
2	tablespoons vegetable oil
2	tablespoons water
1	pound chicken tenders
1	cup cornmeal
2	tablespoons olive oil
½	teaspoon salt
¼	teaspoon pepper

Grate the peel from the lemons and set aside for later. Squeeze the juice from the lemons; you should have about ½ cup of juice. Mix the juice with the tarragon, onion powder, vegetable oil, and water. Place the chicken tenders in a shallow glass dish. Pour the juice mixture over. Cover the dish and marinate in the refrigerator for 4 hours.

Preheat the oven to 400°. Line a cookie sheet or jelly-roll pan with aluminum foil and spray the foil with cooking spray. To prepare the coating for the chicken, mix the cornmeal with the olive oil, 2 teaspoons lemon peel, salt, and pepper. The simplest way to do this is to mix them in a zippered plastic bag and shake it. Then add the chicken tenders to the bag and shake to coat. Place on the prepared pan and bake for 10 minutes. Check for doneness. Don't overcook as they can dry out very easily. Makes 4 servings.

2   cups all-purpose flour
    Grated rind of one
    lemon
2   tablespoons poppy
    seeds
¼   teaspoon salt
½   cup butter
¾   cup sugar
1   egg
½   teaspoon vanilla
    Juice of one lemon plus
    water to equal 3
    tablespoons

Lemon Sandies

On the beautiful Big Island of Hawaii, there are black sand beaches and yellow sand beaches, and these cookies remind me of all of them. The poppy seeds represent the black sand, and the lemon represents the yellow. Aloha!

In a medium bowl mix together the flour, lemon rind, poppy seeds, and salt. In a large bowl cream the butter and sugar until smooth using an electric mixer. Add the egg, vanilla, and lemon juice–water mixture. Add the flour mixture and mix thoroughly. Shape into two rolls that are 1½ inches in diameter. Wrap in waxed paper and chill for 2 hours or overnight.

Preheat the oven to 350°. Slice the rolls in ¼-inch slices and place on a cookie sheet. Bake for 10 minutes. Makes 4 dozen.

Ricotta Cheesecake

A ricotta cheesecake is different from a traditional cheesecake made with cream cheese. It is more delicate and a lot lighter. This lemon version is accented by the subtle flavor of pine nuts. Serve it with freshly sliced strawberries on top for an elegant dessert.

On a baking sheet toast the pine nuts for 10 minutes in a 350° oven. Leave the oven on. Allow the pine nuts to cool. In a blender or food processor mix the pine nuts, cornmeal, flour, butter, and 1 tablespoon sugar until well blended. Reserve 2 tablespoons of the mixture for the top and set aside. Transfer the rest of the mixture to a 9-inch glass pie pan and spread evenly across the bottom, pressing it into the pan.

Rinse the blender or food processor and blend the ricotta, ⅓ cup sugar, egg, lemon rind and juice, and vanilla until very smooth. Pour into the crust. Sprinkle the reserved crumb mixture evenly over the top. Bake for 50 minutes on the middle rack. Serve with sliced berries on top. Makes 6 to 8 servings.

Crust:
- ¼ cup pine nuts
- ½ cup cornmeal
- 2 tablespoons all-purpose flour
- 1 tablespoon butter
- 1 tablespoon sugar

Filling:
- 1 15-ounce container ricotta cheese
- ⅓ cup sugar
- 1 egg
- 1 teaspoon grated lemon rind
- 2 tablespoons lemon juice
- 1 teaspoon vanilla
  Sliced berries for garnish

1   tablespoon olive oil
1   cup chopped onion
1   cup white rice
1¾ cups chicken broth
    Juice and peel of one
    lemon
¼   teaspoon dried dill
    weed
4   fresh dill sprigs
1   tablespoon sugar

Lemon-Dill Rice

*Dill is my favorite herb. It has such a mild flavor that I could
eat it in anything. When combined with the flavor of lemon, it's
a nice balance. This rice dish is great served with grilled salmon
or any type of fish.*

In a Dutch oven or large covered skillet heat the olive oil
and brown the onion. Add the rice and stir for 2 minutes
until the rice grains look opaque but not brown. Add the
broth, lemon peel and juice, dill weed and sprigs, and
sugar. Stir and reduce the heat to medium. Cover and
cook for 15 minutes. Stir again, and then cover and cook
for 10 minutes more or until done. Makes 6 to 8 servings.

Also uses onions

Pork Tagalog

*This is a variation of a dish from the Philippines. It was origi-
nally made with beef, but I adapted it for pork to create a
lighter version. The lemon and onion are a wonderful flavor
combination. Make this in a wok if you have one, but you
could also prepare it in a heavy skillet.*

1	whole lemon
2	teaspoons sesame oil
1	onion, cut in vertical slices
1	teaspoon minced garlic
1	pound pork strips for stir-fry
2	tablespoons all-purpose flour
2	tablespoons soy sauce
	Salt and pepper to taste

While preparing the other ingredients, soak the lemon in a
bowl of hot water; this will bring out the juice. Cut the
lemon in half. Heat the wok over high heat; add the
sesame oil. Stir-fry the onion for 1 to 2 minutes, stirring
to brown evenly. Add the garlic and pork strips and continue to stir-fry for about 5 minutes until the pork is
browned lightly on all sides. Sprinkle the flour over the
mixture and stir to coat. With a meat fork or lemon
juicer, squeeze the juice from the lemon halves into the
wok, then throw the lemon halves in the pan. Add the soy
sauce and stir. Reduce the heat a little and cover the wok.
Cook for 5 or 10 more minutes until the pork is cooked
through. You might want to add a little water if it's sticking. Serve with steamed rice. Makes 4 to 6 servings.

Lemons are very tart and high in acid—two properties that make lemon juice a perfect in-

gredient for marinating any type of meat, chicken, or seafood. Used full strength without

diluting it, a lemon juice marinade tenderizes faster than marinades made with wine or

vinegar. However, you will want to add other flavors when

2 fer For more recipes that
use up lemons, see:

Champagne Roast
Salmon, p. 195

using lemon juice as a marinade; any type of green herb will

add some balance, and so will onions, onion powder, or

garlic. When added to sweet baked goods, lemon juice con-

tributes a light and delicate flavor and texture. When cooking foods

in lemon, you will need other ingredients to balance out the tartness, such as onions or a

little sugar, and you may want to dilute it or the lemon taste will be too strong. The outer-

most layer of the lemon peel is called the zest, and it can be added to baked goods, rice, po-

tatoes, or pasta, to add a hint of tartness and a vibrant color to the food. When the zest is

added to cooked foods, it will also impart a delicate lemon flavor without overpowering

the other flavors.

NOTES

From the kitchen of ——————

From the kitchen of ——————

13
Milk

What's on everybody's grocery list at one time or another? Milk, eggs, and bread. Even the lactose-intolerant can find options these days, with soy milk and rice milk as alternatives. Households with a lot of kids may never have milk left over, but households with just adults may always have a partial carton requiring the sniff test to make sure it's still drinkable. You can sometimes find milk in pints if you only need a little for a recipe, but if you want a certain type such as skim or low-fat, you may be out of luck and find yourself buying more milk than you know you'll ever drink before it expires. Soy milk and rice milk are becoming more common these days, but they can't always be substituted in recipes, especially for things like puddings or anything with gelatin in it, because they won't thicken. The recipes in this chapter have been tested with ordinary cow's milk, unless stated otherwise.

Brownie Pudding Cake

When I was growing up, pudding cakes were all the rage. You could even buy mixes in various flavors. Then they disappeared. I developed this recipe so that you can eat a brownie and some pudding, too. It really does form a brownie on the top of the pudding. When you scoop it out of the pan, you can invert it into a serving dish and have the pudding form a sauce over the top, also. Low-fat or whole milk works best for this recipe; skim milk thins the pudding part too much. It is best served warm.

1	cup all-purpose flour
¼	cup cocoa
¾	cup sugar
2	teaspoons baking powder
1	teaspoon salt
1	cup milk
3	tablespoons vegetable oil
1	teaspoon vanilla
¼	cup sugar
2	tablespoons cocoa
½	cup chopped walnuts
¼	cup chocolate chips
1	cup boiling water

Preheat the oven to 350°. Coat an 8-inch square pan with cooking spray. In a large bowl mix together the flour, ¼ cup cocoa, ¾ cup sugar, baking powder, and salt. Add the milk, vegetable oil, and vanilla, and mix thoroughly. Pour into the prepared pan and spread evenly. In a small bowl mix together ¼ cup sugar and 2 tablespoons cocoa; sprinkle evenly over the mixture. Sprinkle the walnuts and chocolate chips over the batter. Pour the boiling water over the top. Bake for 30 minutes. Serve warm with frozen yogurt or ice cream on top, if desired. Makes 9 servings.

2	cups milk
½	cup sugar
½	teaspoon cinnamon
½	teaspoon salt
½	cup uncooked white rice
1	tablespoon butter
2	eggs
1	teaspoon vanilla
½	cup chopped dates

Oven Rice Pudding

Unlike pudding that's prepared on the stove, this rice pudding has a soufflé-like texture that is created by slowly baking it in the oven. The cinnamon perks up the rice's flavor, and the dates provide a welcome change from the traditional raisins.

In a saucepan combine the milk, sugar, cinnamon, salt, and rice. Bring to a boil, cover, and reduce the heat. Simmer for 15 minutes. Meanwhile, preheat the oven to 325°. Spray a glass casserole dish with cooking spray. Find a larger baking pan that the casserole will fit into because it will bake in a water bath.

Remove the rice mixture from the heat and stir in the butter until it melts. Transfer to the mixing bowl. In a small bowl beat the eggs with the vanilla, then pour slowly into the rice mixture, stirring constantly to avoid setting the eggs. Stir in the dates. Pour into the prepared pan and set it inside the larger pan. Pour hot water into the outer pan so that the water is one inch high. Bake for 45 minutes. Allow to cool for 15 minutes. Serve while still warm. Makes 6 servings.

Scalloped Parsley Potatoes

This easy potato dish takes the best of the starch from the potatoes and the liquid of the milk to create a creamy texture. Shallots and parsley add just enough subtle flavor to this delicate dish.

2	tablespoons butter
2	large or 4 medium Idaho potatoes
	Salt and pepper to taste
2	shallots, minced
2	tablespoons fresh parsley
2	tablespoons all-purpose flour
1	cup milk

Preheat the oven to 350°. Place 1 tablespoon butter in a 1½-quart casserole dish and put it in the oven to melt the butter. Brush the butter up the sides of the dish, coating the interior surface. Slice the potatoes very thin; you can peel them or leave the skin, whichever you prefer. Place one-third of the potato slices in the casserole, followed by salt and pepper, one-third of the shallots, one-third of the parsley, and one-third of the flour. Repeat the layers twice more, ending with the flour. Pour the milk into the casserole at the side so that it doesn't wash away the top layer of flour. Dot with the remaining butter. Cover the dish. Bake for 45 minutes, then uncover and bake for 15 more minutes. Makes 4 to 6 servings.

Also uses potatoes

2   eggs
1   cup milk
1   teaspoon vanilla
¼   cup butter, melted
2   cups whole-wheat flour
½   cup sugar
1   tablespoon baking
    powder
½   teaspoon baking soda
½   teaspoon salt
1   cup fresh or frozen
    cranberries, chopped
½   cup chopped pecans

Cranberry Muffins

Muffins are a great way to use up milk, and they're fast to make. These are the traditional muffins I make on Thanksgiving morning, to eat while the turkey is roasting. They are best made with fresh cranberries, but you can use dried cranberries that have been soaked in warm water for 10 minutes.

Preheat the oven to 375°. Grease the tins of a muffin pan or use paper muffin cups. In a large mixing bowl blend the eggs, milk, vanilla, and melted butter. In a separate mixing bowl, blend the flour, sugar, baking powder, soda, and salt. Add the egg mixture to the dry ingredients and stir until blended. Stir in the cranberries and nuts. Spoon into the prepared muffin tins. Bake for 22 minutes. Makes 12 muffins.

Oven Pancake

Making a large pancake in the oven is a lot easier than making lots of small ones. The nice thing about pancakes is that they use a lot of milk. This pancake gets crispy and buttery on the bottom. I like to serve it with fresh sliced strawberries for brunch.

1	tablespoon butter
3	eggs
¾	cup milk
¾	cup all-purpose flour
1	teaspoon vanilla
1	tablespoon sugar

Preheat the oven to 425°. You will need either a 10-inch cast iron skillet that you can use in the oven or a 12-inch paella pan. Place the butter in the pan and let it melt while the oven is heating up. In a mixing bowl blend the eggs, milk, flour, vanilla, and sugar. Using potholders, remove the pan from the oven and swirl the butter around so that it coats the pan. Pour the mixture into the pan. Bake for 20 minutes, then reduce the oven temperature to 350° and bake until set. Remove from the oven and serve. Makes 4 to 6 servings.

Also uses eggs

The thing to remember about using up milk is that if it is nearing the expiration date, you will want to use it in a recipe that is cooked or baked. Lots of different baked goods require milk, and most layer cakes require at least a cup or more of milk, depending on the size. So, when you have milk left over, get out your favorite cake recipe and let 'em eat cake! A lot of yeast breads also use milk as the liquid, which gives the bread a softer texture. Puddings that are cooked on top of the stove or baked are another good way to use milk. You can use it to cook starches such as rice or potatoes, add it to eggs for scrambled eggs or French toast, or make pancakes. Most milk recipes are for baked goods or with starches; it doesn't work well with meats, poultry, or seafood unless you add it to a soup as part of the liquid; in that case, it can take the place of cream in the soup.

2 fer

For more recipes that use up milk, see:

Inside-Out Breakfast, p. 67
Baklava Twists, p. 75
Berriest Smoothie, p. 87
Luau Pudding, p. 157

NOTES

From the kitchen of —————

From the kitchen of —————

14
Olives

Raise your hand, everyone who has a partial jar of olives in your refrigerator! Because by their very nature olives are already preserved, we tend to hold on to them for a long, long time. Olives are one of those condiments that are very pungent and salty, and it doesn't take much to lend a strong flavor to a dish. If olives are eaten plain or with appetizers, most people don't eat more than 3 or 4 at a time. There are multitudes of different ways of preserving olives, but there are two basic types: green and black. Green olives may be brined or preserved with olive oil and herbs, or may be stuffed with almonds or pimentos. Black olives may be oil-cured or brine-cured, and may be prepared with herbs and spices. These days, many supermarkets or gourmet markets have various types of olives that can be purchased in bulk, but the more common packaging is in jars or cans. Many olives are imported, although there are also many domestic olives.

Snapper Veracruz

Even people who aren't fish fans will find this recipe tasty and appealing. White-fleshed fish, such as snapper, cod, and redfish, can sometimes be bland. The spices in this dish liven up the flavor and enhance the delicate texture of the fish. You can use any type of firm white-fleshed fish in this recipe.

1½	pounds red snapper fillets
½	teaspoon oregano
½	teaspoon ground cumin
3	tablespoons olive oil
½	cup chopped onion
1	teaspoon minced garlic
½	cup sliced black olives (can use a few green also)
1	tablespoon lemon juice
1	tablespoon capers
¼	cup red wine
1	cup chopped tomatoes

Preheat the oven to 400°. Spray a 9 x 13-inch baking dish with cooking spray. Cut the fish into serving pieces. In a small bowl blend the oregano and cumin and sprinkle over the fish. In a skillet heat 2 tablespoons olive oil and sauté the fish pieces. Place the pieces in the prepared baking dish. In the same sauté pan, add 1 tablespoon olive oil and add the onion, garlic, and olives. Sauté for 2 minutes until the onion is soft. Add the lemon juice, capers, wine, and tomatoes to the pan. Cook for 5 minutes over medium high heat. Pour the mixture over the fish. Cover with foil and bake for 15 minutes. Makes 6 servings.

3   cups bread flour
1   tablespoon instant yeast
½   teaspoon oregano
¼   cup olive oil
1   cup warm water at
    "bread" temperature
    (105 degrees)
¼   cup finely chopped
    green or black olives

Topping:
    Olive oil for brushing
    Cracked pepper
¼   cup olives, cut into
    slivers
2   tablespoons chopped
    parsley

Olive Focaccia

Focaccia is a very versatile bread that can be flavored with almost anything and topped with almost anything. You can use focaccia to make sandwiches, serve it as an accompaniment to salads or soups, or just eat it as an appetizer. This one features olives in a starring role.

In a large bowl mix together 2 cups flour, the yeast, and oregano, and stir until blended. Add ¼ cup olive oil and mix well. Add the water and stir, then add the chopped olives and stir again. Add enough of the remaining flour and stir until it leaves the sides of the bowl. Turn out onto a floured board and knead until smooth and elastic. Place in an oiled bowl, cover with a towel, and allow to rise for 20 minutes or until double.

Preheat the oven to 400°. Spray a 9 x 13-inch pan with cooking spray. Transfer the dough to a floured board and roll out to the approximate size of the pan. Place the dough in the pan and pat it into the bottom in an even layer. Brush with olive oil. Sprinkle with a little cracked pepper, then the slivered olives, and then the parsley. Press down lightly into the dough. Let rise for 10 minutes. Bake on the center rack for 20 minutes. Remove from the oven and brush lightly with olive oil again. Makes 8 to 10 servings.

Pork Tenderloins with Olive Wine Sauce

Many types of meats or poultry are available in the form of tenderloins, which are slices that are usually about ¼ inch thick. The nice thing is, they don't take long to cook, so they're great to have on hand for a quick meal. This recipe uses pork tenderloins, which are really boneless loin pork chops. The olives and the wine go nicely with the pork. Great served with polenta or pasta.

On a paper plate mix together the flour, thyme, and salt. Dredge the pork chops in this mixture and set aside. In a large skillet heat the olive oil and brown the pork chops, turning once. Remove to a platter. In the same skillet sauté the garlic and oregano, and add the wine. Cook for 2 to 3 minutes until it starts to glaze. Add the broth, tomatoes, and olives, and allow the sauce to cook for 2 minutes more. Return the pork chops to the pan and heat through until the pork chops are fully cooked, about 1 more minute. To serve, place some sauce on top of each pork chop and sprinkle with parsley. Makes 4 to 8 servings.

2   tablespoons all-purpose flour
1   teaspoon thyme
1   teaspoon salt
2   tablespoons olive oil
8   pork tenderloins

Sauce:
1   teaspoon minced garlic
½   teaspoon oregano
¼   cup white wine
¼   cup chicken broth
2   Roma tomatoes, diced
10 chopped green or black olives
    Fresh parsley for garnish

1   large eggplant, cut into
    1-inch slices
1   tablespoon olive oil
¾   cup finely diced celery
½   cup finely chopped
    onion
1   teaspoon minced garlic
3   Roma tomatoes,
    chopped
4   tablespoons tomato
    sauce
2   tablespoons wine
    vinegar
3   tablespoons chopped
    black olives
1   tablespoon capers
1   teaspoon sugar
    Fresh parsley for garnish

Caponata

About ten years ago, it was easy to find cans of this great little appetizer in the supermarket, then they disappeared from the shelves. I used to love caponata because it was a great addition to an appetizer tray, and was wonderful served on bread, crackers or pita bread. Once you make this, you will be hooked. It lasts for a week in the refrigerator and makes a lot. It's also very low in calories!

Preheat the oven to 425°. Place the eggplant on a large cookie sheet lined with aluminum foil. Spray with olive oil–flavored cooking spray. Bake for 15 minutes or until soft. Allow to cool. Dice the eggplant into ½-inch pieces. In a large skillet heat the olive oil and brown the celery, onion, and garlic. Sauté for 5 minutes until golden. Add the tomatoes and sauce, vinegar, olives, capers, and sugar, and reduce the heat to low. Cover the skillet and cook for 10 minutes. Add the eggplant and stir well to blend. Cover again and cook for 5 minutes more. Spoon into a glass bowl or serving dish and refrigerate. About 1 hour before serving, remove from the refrigerator to warm to room temperature. Serve on thin slices of French bread or crackers, and garnish with parsley. Makes 3 to 4 cups.

Also uses tomatoes

Salad Nicoise

This is one of my favorite salads because it has several of my favorite foods: potatoes, green beans, and olives. For a variation, try fresh tuna that has been grilled and then cut into strips. Nice salad to serve outside on a sunny day.

12	small red potatoes
½	pound green beans
8	ounces fresh spinach leaves
1	head butter lettuce
2	6-ounce cans tuna, drained
24	black olives (with or without pits)
12	radishes, halved
2	tablespoons chopped parsley

Dressing:

¼	cup olive oil
2	tablespoons rice vinegar
1	tablespoon water
½	teaspoon Dijon mustard

Quarter the red potatoes. In a saucepan with a steamer basket steam them for about 20 minutes or until cooked through but not mushy. Drain and rinse in a colander with cold water. Cut the green beans into 1-inch pieces. Cook in boiling water for 8 minutes and drain; rinse with cold water. Take four salad serving plates and divide up the spinach and butter lettuce to form a bed for the salad. Arrange the rest of the ingredients in an attractive design on each plate. I usually put the tuna in the middle, surrounded by the green beans, then the potatoes, then the olives and radishes alternating around the edge. In a medium bowl whisk together the ingredients for the dressing and drizzle over the top of each salad. Sprinkle with parsley and serve. Makes 4 main-dish servings.

Working with olives means that first you must remove the pits, unless you bought them already pitted. You can use a cherry pitter to do this, and there is a gadget that is called an olive pitter that looks the same. Once the olives are pitted, you will use them either whole, in slivers, or chopped. Look for recipes where little bits of olives could be used to provide pungent flavor to other ingredients in a dish, like vegetable or potato salads, pastas, or soups. Any type of pizza dish can use a few olives in it or on it. Olives work well with fish, poultry, and some meats. Chopped olives can be used in Mexican dishes such as burritos, enchiladas, or tacos. Olives can be added to tomato-based sauces and provide a pungent flavor. Start by adding a small amount of olives to the dish, and then taste it before adding more. A few olives also make a nice garnish for salads or entrées.

NOTES

From the kitchen of _____

From the kitchen of _____

15
Onions

No matter how few or how many onions I buy at a time, there always seems to be one that begins to sprout. Why is it always the biggest one? Onions take up a lot of room and I have a pretty small refrigerator, so I tend to keep them in a dry, relatively cool place instead, but there are always two or three that need to be cooked right away. The most common onions used in cooking are yellow onions that are three to five inches in diameter. They are sold by the pound or in five- or ten-pound bags. White onions are hotter, and I rarely use them. Red or purple onions are also available, but their strong flavor and color work only in limited dishes. In most dishes, onions are either sliced or chopped and used as one flavoring ingredient in a dish. But onions are also a vegetable unto themselves, and that's one of the best ways to use up onions.

Summer Squash with Slow-Cooked Onions

Slow-cooked onions add a special flavor to any dish. Sautéing onions slowly in a pan over very low heat results in a sweet, golden brown treasure. Because summer squash can be bland by itself, the toasted onion flavor transforms the squash into a succulent side dish.

2	tablespoons olive oil
1	yellow onion, cut thinly into horizontal slices
2	teaspoons olive oil
5	to 6 zucchini or other summer squash, cut into ½-inch slices
½	teaspoon oregano
2	tablespoons water

In a heavy sauté pan heat 2 tablespoons olive oil and add the onion slices. Over medium heat, brown the onions slightly, then reduce the heat to low. Cook for about 10 minutes total, stirring occasionally. Remove from the pan and cool. Add 2 teaspoons olive oil to the sauté pan, then add the squash and sprinkle with oregano. Sauté for about 5 minutes over medium high heat. Add the water, cover, and reduce the heat to medium. Cook for 5 minutes. Add the onions to the squash and stir to heat through. Makes 6 servings.

3 cups unbleached flour or bread flour

1 tablespoon instant yeast

1 teaspoon salt

½ teaspoon onion powder

1 cup warm water

2 teaspoons olive oil

1 teaspoon dried rosemary

½ cup finely chopped yellow onion

Onion-Rosemary Bread

This is a wonderful crusty loaf on the outside, with a sweet soft texture on the inside. The rosemary in the dough adds just a hint of savoriness. Makes a wonderful sandwich bread for turkey or roast beef.

In the bowl of a stand mixer blend 2 cups flour, the yeast, salt, and onion powder. Heat the water to 105° and add to the bowl with the olive oil. Beat for about 5 minutes, until the dough is mixed thoroughly. Add the rosemary and beat once again until distributed throughout the dough. Turn out onto a floured board and add the remaining cup of flour, working in the flour as you knead the dough. When the dough is elastic, place in an oiled bowl, cover, and let rise for about 30 minutes, until doubled.

Remove the dough to a floured board. Preheat the oven to 400°. If you have a bread stone or a pizza stone, place in the oven before preheating. Sprinkle a cookie sheet with cornmeal. Punch down the dough and roll it out into a 10 x 14-inch rectangle. Sprinkle the chopped onion evenly over the dough. Roll up from the 14-inch side, and pinch the edges to seal. Place on the prepared cookie sheet. Cover the loaf with a towel and let rise in a warm place until doubled, about 30 minutes. With a sharp knife, cut 3 or 4 slits diagonally across the loaf. Place the cookie sheet in the oven or transfer the loaf to the bread stone. Bake for 5 minutes, then spray the loaf with water. Return to the oven and reduce the oven temperature to 350°. Bake for 20 more minutes, or until the loaf sounds hollow when tapped. Makes one long loaf of bread that serves 8 to 10.

Oven-Roasted Winter Vegetables

There's nothing like a pan of vegetables roasting in the oven to perk up an appetite. Onions not only serve as another vegetable in this dish, but also add a wonderful flavor to the other root vegetables. If you've never tried kohlrabi, you might be in for a pleasant surprise. In the store, it looks like a large light green turnip. It has a delicate flavor like water chestnuts. If you can't find kohlrabi, you can substitute turnips, rutabagas, or even Brussels sprouts.

1	or 2 whole onions
4	carrots
3	parsnips
2	kohlrabis
2	tablespoons olive oil
½	teaspoon thyme
1	teaspoon minced garlic
½	teaspoon paprika

Preheat the oven to 375°. Line a shallow roasting pan with aluminum foil and spray with cooking spray. To prepare the vegetables, cut the onions into 1-inch chunks. Peel the carrots, parsnips, and kohlrabis. Cut the carrots and parsnips into ½-inch slices. Cut the kohlrabis in half, then cut into ¼-inch slices. In a large mixing bowl toss all of the vegetables with the olive oil, thyme, garlic, and paprika until evenly coated. Transfer to the roasting pan and roast for 1 hour. Cover the pan with foil and roast for 15 more minutes, until the carrots are cooked through. Makes 8 to 10 servings.

Also uses carrots

2	tablespoons all-purpose flour
½	teaspoon paprika
½	teaspoon salt
3	tablespoons olive oil
2	large onions
1	3-pound chuck or rump roast
4	medium-sized potatoes
4	carrots
½	to 1 cup beef broth

Onion-Smothered Pot Roast

Pot roast just wouldn't be pot roast without onions. This is a different way of cooking it, with the onions all around it. You can make this in a crock pot or in the oven.

In a small bowl mix together the flour, paprika, and salt and spread over the outside of the roast. In a large skillet heat 1 tablespoon olive oil and brown the roast lightly on all sides. Set aside. Rinse the skillet. Cut the onions into thin vertical slices. Place in the skillet with 2 tablespoons olive oil and slow-cook the onions over medium low heat for about 15 minutes, until golden brown but not dark. Place half of the onions in the bottom of a Dutch oven (or in a crock pot). Place the roast on top of the onions. Peel the potatoes and cut into quarters or eighths, depending on size. Peel and cut the carrots into 1-inch pieces. Place the carrots and potatoes around the roast. Place the remaining onions over the top, then pour the broth along the side. Cover the Dutch oven and roast at 325° for 1 hour and 30 minutes, or until the potatoes are done. If using a crock pot, cook over low heat for 8 hours. Makes 8 servings.

Also uses carrots

Ratatouille Sandwiches

The flavors of ratatouille combine with sausages in this colorful sandwich. You can use cooked Italian sausages or any type of smoked chicken or turkey sausage. Serve on French rolls. Great for a tailgate party or casual lunch.

In a large skillet heat the olive oil and brown the pepper, onion, garlic, eggplants, and mushrooms for 5 minutes over medium high heat. Sprinkle with the parsley, oregano, and basil, and stir to distribute evenly. Add the tomatoes and sausage pieces and cook for about 5 more minutes or until the tomatoes release their juice and the mixture sticks together. Spoon into French rolls and serve. Makes 6 servings.

1 tablespoon olive oil

1 red bell pepper, julienned

1 yellow onion, sliced thin

2 teaspoons garlic

2 small Japanese eggplants, cut into ½-inch slices

1 cup thinly sliced mushrooms

1 teaspoon fresh parsley

1 teaspoon fresh oregano

1 teaspoon fresh basil (or ¼ teaspoon dried)

3 Roma tomatoes, chopped

6 turkey smoked sausages (fully cooked) sliced into 1-inch pieces

6 French rolls

Also uses tomatoes

Onions are sweet and savory at the same time.

Cooking onions releases the sweetness to the

other ingredients in the dish, making them a

good balancing ingredient for tart foods such

as tomatoes, olives, citrus, wine, or vinegar.

The savory flavor blends well with vegetables

of any kind when cooked together. When

2 *fer* For more recipes that use up onions, see:

Brown Rice Jambalaya, p. 63
Lemon-Dill Rice, p. 94
Cha Cha Chili, p. 179
Flash Minestrone, p. 187
Saucy Oven Pork Chops, p. 188
Champagne Roast Salmon, p. 195

adding onions to a dish, they will have more flavor if you sauté them in olive

oil or butter first before adding them to a soup, stew, or sauce. When adding onions to

baked goods, such as bread or biscuits, be aware that onions will stay very wet in the bread

and may create little holes or pockets; if that is not the desired result, you might want to

reconsider.

NOTES

From the kitchen of _____

From the kitchen of _____

16
Orange Juice

Freshly squeezed orange juice, direct from the orchard to your grocer's refrigerator to your refrigerator. That's the best way to drink it, but it doesn't last forever. Orange juice is most commonly packaged in one-quart or half-gallon cartons these days. Orange juice made from frozen concentrate still makes a very large pitcher, at least 48 ounces. The typical serving is 4 or 8 ounces, so unless many people in the household drink it every day, there will likely be some left. Luckily, orange juice is the least tart of the citrus juices, and its natural sweetness makes it ideal for lots of different recipes. So, no, orange juice is not just for breakfast anymore.

Orange-Blueberry Bread

Oranges and blueberries together are a striking color contrast, and they make this bread beautiful to look at. Of course, their flavors are wonderful together, too; so don't stare at it too long! This is a moist bread that freezes well and is great for brunch or a snack.

½	cup butter
⅔	cup sugar
1	egg
1	teaspoon vanilla
1	cup orange juice
2	cups all-purpose flour
¼	teaspoon salt
1	teaspoon baking powder
½	teaspoon baking soda
1	cup blueberries (fresh or frozen)

Syrup:

½	cup orange juice
¼	cup sugar

Preheat the oven to 350°. Spray a 4 x 8-inch loaf pan with cooking spray. In a large mixing bowl cream together the butter and sugar. Add the egg, vanilla, and orange juice. In a separate bowl mix together the flour, salt, baking powder, and soda, then add to the wet ingredients. Mix thoroughly. Stir in the blueberries. Bake on the middle rack for 1 hour.

Remove the bread from the oven, and let cool in the pan for 10 minutes. Meanwhile, make the syrup. In a saucepan combine the orange juice and sugar. Bring to a boil and cook for 1 minute. Remove from the heat. Poke holes in the bread with a thin skewer or meat fork. Pour the syrup over and allow the bread to cool completely before removing from the pan. Makes 12 servings.

1   cup orange juice
½   teaspoon minced garlic
2   tablespoons sesame oil
½   teaspoon onion powder
½   teaspoon basil
1   pound large prawns,
    shelled and deveined
1   bunch asparagus
8   ounces fresh spinach

Orange-Basil Prawn Salad

Citrus and seafood just go together. Lemon and lime are often used with seafood, but for a change, try oranges. This is a wonderful main-dish salad.

In a medium bowl mix together the orange juice, garlic, oil, onion powder, and basil. Pour the mixture over the prawns and marinate in a shallow glass dish in the refrigerator for 3 to 4 hours. Meanwhile, cut the asparagus into 1-inch pieces and cook in boiling water for 3 minutes. Drain in a colander and rinse in cold water.

Drain the prawns. In a medium skillet heat a little olive oil and sauté the prawns. Add the asparagus and toss to coat. Serve on a bed of spinach on salad plates. Makes 4 appetizer servings or 2 main-dish servings.

Orange Chiffon

This is a very light and refreshing dessert, perfect after a some-what heavy meal or with an outdoor barbecue. Beware; this is addictive, and people might be asking for seconds.

2	cups graham cracker crumbs
¼	cup melted butter
4	egg yolks
1	cup sugar
1	envelope unflavored gelatin
1	cup orange juice
4	egg whites
½	cup sugar
2	cups Cool Whip or prepared whipped cream

In a medium bowl mix the graham cracker crumbs and butter, and place half the mixture in the bottom of a 9 x 13-inch pan, reserving the rest of the crumbs for the top. In the top of a double boiler place the egg yolks and 1 cup sugar. Cook over boiling water until thick. Dissolve the unflavored gelatin in the orange juice. Add to the mixture in the double boiler and cook, stirring constantly, for about 3 minutes. Remove from the heat. In a large mixing bowl beat the egg whites and ½ cup sugar until stiff. With a spatula, fold in the orange juice mixture and stir until smooth. Fold in the Cool Whip or whipped cream until the consistency is very smooth. Pour into the prepared pan, and smooth the top. Sprinkle the rest of the graham cracker crumbs on the top. Chill until set. Makes 10 to 12 servings.

Also uses eggs

Spice mixture: ⅛
teaspoon ginger, ¼
teaspoon onion
powder, ⅛ teaspoon
salt, ⅛ teaspoon pepper

4   chicken breast halves
1   tablespoon olive oil
½   cup orange juice

Basting sauce:

2   tablespoons orange
     liqueur, such as
     Cointreau, or brandy
1   tablespoon brown sugar
¼   teaspoon marjoram
½   cup orange juice
1   tablespoon cornstarch,
     mixed in 2 tablespoons
     cold water

Chicken à l'Orange

*Orange sauce is classically used on roasted duck, but it tastes
just great on ordinary chicken, too. This recipe was designed
for chicken breasts. If you decide to use chicken legs or thighs,
you will need to roast them longer.*

Preheat the oven to 350°. Blend together the spices, and
rub over the chicken. In a large skillet heat the olive oil
and brown the chicken briefly. Place the chicken on the
rack of a roasting pan. Pour ½ cup orange juice over the
chicken.

   In a saucepan mix together the liqueur, brown sugar,
marjoram, and orange juice. Cook over medium high heat
until the mixture comes to a boil. Add the cornstarch-
water mixture and stir until thickened. Remove from the
heat. Baste the chicken with the sauce. Roast for 30 minutes, then baste once more and roast for 15 more minutes.
Makes 4 servings.

Ambrosia Cupcakes

Oranges and coconut are classic ingredients in the fruit salad known as ambrosia. These delicate cupcakes combine these wonderful flavors. If you desire a more intense orange flavor, add 2 teaspoons of grated orange peel to the cupcake batter.

Preheat the oven to 350°. Prepare a 12-cup muffin or cupcake pan by lining with paper muffin cups. In a large mixing bowl cream together the melted butter and sugar. Place the egg whites in a separate bowl. Add the egg yolk to the butter and sugar mixture, and add the almond extract, orange juice, and liqueur. Beat well. Add the flour, baking powder, and salt, and blend again. Add the coconut and blend until distributed. Beat the egg whites until stiff. Fold into the batter. Spoon into the prepared cupcake tin. Bake for 20 minutes on the middle rack.

To make the frosting, in a small bowl mix together 1 cup powdered sugar and 2 tablespoons butter. Mix in 1 tablespoon orange juice and blend. Spread on the cooled cupcakes. Makes 12 cupcakes.

¼ cup melted butter
⅔ cup sugar
1 egg white
1 egg, separated
½ teaspoon almond extract
½ cup orange juice
1 tablespoon orange liqueur such as Grand Marnier or Cointreau
1¼ cups cake flour
2 teaspoons baking powder
¼ teaspoon salt
½ cup unsweetened shredded coconut

Orange buttercream frosting:
1 cup confectioners' sugar
2 tablespoons butter
1 tablespoon orange juice

To use up orange juice, you will need to use it in recipes that require a cup or more of liquid. Most cake and bread recipes call for at least a cup of liquid, so they are natural candidates. Some sauces and most marinades need lots of liquids, and the tart sweetness of orange juice will blend well with herbs, spices, and seasonings. The flavor of orange blends well with tropical fruits, such as bananas, pineapples, mangoes, or papayas, so using orange juice as a fruit salad dressing would work well. Keep in mind that orange juice will have a more subtle flavor in baked goods than if you used the orange peel or zest; if you're looking for a more pungent flavor, you might want to add some orange zest to the orange juice for a flavor boost.

NOTES

From the kitchen of ——————

From the kitchen of ——————

17
Peas (Frozen)

I know a lot of people who keep bags of frozen peas for medicinal purposes—they make a great flexible cold compress for sore muscles, joints, or even for headaches. The rest of us buy a bag of peas, use half a cup, and then wait until the rest have too much freezer burn to taste good. Then we toss them out. Well, it's time to stop neglecting those peas in the freezer. They are vibrant in color, fast to cook, and you can do lots of things with them. Frozen peas are packaged in either 8-ounce or 1-pound bags, or in small wax boxes. They come in two different sizes; regular- and "petite"-sized peas that have a more delicate flavor. Peas are meant to be served as a vegetable by itself, but they can be awfully bland. They become more flavorful and interesting when mixed with vegetables and meats, or as the basis for a soup or stew. This chapter features some new ways to add peas to your cooking repertoire.

Turkey Stew

Turkey and sweet potatoes just go together. This stew is also a colorful mix, with the green of the peas and beans, and the orange of the sweet potatoes.

In a plastic bag, place the flour, salt, and pepper. Add the turkey pieces and shake to coat. In a Dutch oven heat the olive oil and sauté the turkey pieces over medium high heat for about 8 minutes, until browned. Remove from the pan. In the same pan combine the sweet potatoes, onion, green beans, and salt, and sauté for about 5 minutes. Return the turkey to the pan. Add the chicken broth, cover, and cook for 15 minutes at medium heat. Add the peas and cook for 5 more minutes. Add the cornstarch-water mixture and stir to thicken. Makes 6 to 8 hearty servings.

¼ cup all-purpose flour
½ teaspoon salt
¼ teaspoon pepper
1 pound turkey cutlets, cut into cubes
2 teaspoons olive oil
2 sweet potatoes, peeled and diced
1 large onion, diced
1 cup green beans, cut into 1-inch pieces
½ teaspoon salt
2 cups chicken broth
1 cup frozen peas
1 tablespoon cornstarch mixed with 2 tablespoons water

1½ cups peas

¼ cup mayonnaise

1 teaspoon Worcestershire sauce

1 teaspoon sugar

½ cup unsalted roasted Virginia peanuts

¼ cup minced celery

2 green onions, cut into thin slices

Pea and Peanut Salad

This unusual salad is high in protein, and the combination is delightful. The soft crunch of the peanuts and celery adds contrast to the soft and tasty peas.

Thaw the peas in the microwave for 1 to 2 minutes on medium. In a small bowl whisk together the mayonnaise, Worcestershire, and sugar until smooth. In a medium bowl stir together the peas, peanuts, celery, and green onion. Pour on the dressing and blend well. Refrigerate for 1 to 2 hours to blend the flavors. Makes 4 to 6 servings.

Double Pea Soup

Combining dried split peas with bright frozen peas makes a hearty soup with a pleasing green color. Using the yam adds a little sweetness for a very pleasing taste.

1	tablespoon olive oil
2	cloves garlic, minced
2	stalks celery, chopped
1	yam, peeled and diced
1	medium onion, chopped
2	cups split peas, soaked overnight in water
2	quarts water
½	teaspoon marjoram
1	teaspoon basil
½	teaspoon cumin
2	cups frozen peas
4	slices Canadian bacon, diced

In a skillet heat the olive oil and sauté the garlic, celery, yam, and onion for 5 minutes. In a soup pot place the drained split peas, water, and sautéed vegetables. Add the marjoram, basil, and cumin. Bring to a boil, then lower the heat and simmer for 45 minutes, stirring every 15 minutes to prevent the peas from sticking. Cook the frozen peas in a small amount of water in a saucepan for 2 minutes. Drain, then purée in a blender along with 2 cups of the soup from the pot. Add to the soup pot. Add the Canadian bacon and simmer for 5 more minutes. Add salt to taste. If the soup is too thick, add a little water to achieve the desired consistency. Makes 3 quarts.

1   tablespoon olive oil
½   cup chopped onion
¼   cup chopped celery
½   cup sliced mushrooms
1   cup rice
2   cups chicken broth
¼   teaspoon dill weed
¼   teaspoon paprika
1   cup frozen peas

Rice Pilaf with Peas and Mushrooms

Rice pilaf is a staple at our house. It's a versatile side dish that goes with just about anything. This version is dressed up with peas and mushrooms, which makes it very colorful.

In a large saucepan heat the olive oil and brown the onion and celery over medium high heat. Sauté for 2 or 3 minutes, until the onion is golden. Add the mushrooms and sauté for 2 more minutes. Add the rice and cook, stirring constantly, until the rice grains are opaque but not brown. Add the chicken broth, dill weed, and paprika. Reduce the heat to medium low and cover. Cook for 15 minutes, then add the peas. Cook for 10 more minutes and serve. Makes 6 to 8 servings.

Pasta Peasto

One of the great things about peas is that they are easy to purée. Therefore, they can provide a base for soup or sauce. In this unusual recipe, they form the base for a vividly colored pasta sauce.

1	cup frozen peas
1	teaspoon minced garlic
½	cup chicken broth
½	cup water
1	tablespoon olive oil
2	teaspoons olive oil
2	tablespoons pine nuts
1	cup sliced mushrooms
¼	teaspoon basil
¼	teaspoon oregano
½	teaspoon salt
1	cup artichoke hearts, quartered
¼	cup white wine
	Hot cooked linguine for 4 people

In a medium saucepan cook the peas with the garlic, broth, and water for 5 minutes. Transfer to a blender or food processor, add 1 tablespoon olive oil, and purée until the peas are very smooth and creamy. Return the mixture to the saucepan. In a medium skillet heat 2 teaspoons olive oil and sauté the pine nuts for about 3 minutes, until golden brown. Remove the pine nuts from the skillet and set aside. Add the mushrooms to the skillet and sprinkle with basil, oregano, and salt. Sauté for about 3 minutes, until the mushrooms release their moisture. Add the artichoke hearts and wine, and cook for 2 minutes. Pour the mixture into the saucepan with peas and stir all together. Stir in the pine nuts to distribute. Serve over linguine. Makes 4 servings.

Peas are a starchy vegetable, so when puréed they have thickening properties. Puréed cooked peas added to a soup or sauce will result in a creamy texture without adding cream. If frozen peas are cooked too long, they will lose their vibrant color and look unappetizing. Frozen peas will be fully cooked in 5 minutes or less, so if you will be adding them to recipes in which other ingredients take a longer time to cook, add the peas at the very end to preserve the color and prevent overcooking.

For more recipes that use up peas, see:

Shepherd's Pie, p. 140

Peas have a very mild flavor, so they blend well with more pungent flavors such as tomatoes, wine, or herbs. They are also quite filling because they are so starchy, so you probably won't want to add them to a dish that is already very heavy.

NOTES

From the kitchen of

From the kitchen of

18
Potatoes

I just love potatoes in any shape or form, but my husband has a slight allergy to them. Therefore, I always seem to have a few potatoes that begin to sprout or start to look a little withered. Potatoes are most often stored in a cool, dry place, but not in the refrigerator because they take up way too much room. Unfortunately, that also means they can sprout or become withered or dry. When they're in that state, they either need to be peeled completely, or the withered spots need to be cut off. There are many new varieties of potatoes available on the market today, including exotic varieties such as purple potatoes, Yellow Finn, and Yukon Gold, as well as the old standard Idaho bakers and red potatoes. Whatever variety you have will work in most of these recipes.

Potato-Leek Soup

Potatoes and leeks are a natural combination in the classic soup vichyssoise. Most of the time, milk or cream is added to the soup as well. I prefer a lighter version without milk that makes use of the creamy nature of potatoes. By puréeing some of the cooked potatoes and adding it back to the soup, you get the same consistency as a cream soup without the calories.

3 cups peeled and diced potatoes, any kind

2 leeks, chopped

1 quart chicken broth

1 teaspoon dried dill weed

½ teaspoon salt

⅛ teaspoon white pepper

In a soup pot combine all of the ingredients. Bring to a boil, then simmer, covered, for 30 minutes. Remove about half of the soup and purée in a blender or food processor. Return the puréed mixture to the soup pot and stir. Makes 4 to 6 servings.

3   large or 6 medium
    potatoes
2   teaspoons butter
1   tablespoon olive oil
1   pound ground turkey
¼   cup minced celery
½   cup chopped onion
¾   cup beef broth
1   tablespoon catsup
¼   teaspoon dry mustard
1   teaspoon
    Worcestershire sauce
½   cup uncooked peas
    (fresh or frozen)
    Paprika for garnish

Shepherd's Pie

Mashed potatoes make a great topping for casseroles, and Shepherd's Pie is a classic. This version uses ground turkey, but you can also use ground beef. The peas add another color and some variety to the dish. You can make individual pies in little foil tart pans instead of one big dish, also.

Preheat the oven to 400°. Dice the potatoes and place in a saucepan, then add water to cover. Cook for 15 minutes and drain, reserving ¼ cup of the potato water. Mash the potatoes, adding 2 teaspoons butter and enough of the reserved potato water to create a smooth texture.

In a skillet heat the olive oil and sauté the turkey, celery, and onion until the turkey is brown. Add the broth, catsup, mustard, and Worcestershire. Cook for 5 minutes. Add the peas and stir to distribute. Transfer the mixture to an 8-inch square baking pan. Spread the potatoes in an even layer over top. Sprinkle with paprika. Bake for 30 minutes on the center rack. (If using tart pans, bake for 15 minutes.) Makes 6 servings.

Also uses peas

Roasted Garlic Potatoes

Potatoes are my favorite side dish. This recipe is great with any kind of potato, but I like to use some of the newer varieties, such as purple or yellow potatoes.

12 small or 8 medium-
    sized potatoes
12 cloves of garlic
½   teaspoon dill weed
2   tablespoons olive oil
    Cracked pepper
    Salt to taste

Preheat the oven to 400°. Line a 9 x 13-inch baking pan with aluminum foil and brush with olive oil. Remove any sprouts or dark spots from the potatoes with a paring knife. Quarter the potatoes and place in a mixing bowl. Peel the garlic cloves and cut into slivers; add to the mixing bowl. Sprinkle the dill weed over the potatoes and toss. Add the olive oil to the bowl and toss to coat. Put the potatoes in the prepared pan, and heap them up so that some garlic is touching each potato. Sprinkle with cracked pepper and a little salt. Roast for 45 minutes or until fork-tender. Makes 6 servings.

4 large potatoes
4 ounces flaked smoked
   chunk salmon or lox
2 tablespoons butter
¼ teaspoon paprika
   Salt to taste

Alsatian Potato Pancake

I had this delightful dish in a restaurant in northern England, where the chef was Alsatian and the owner was British. I never did get the recipe, but I came home and experimented until I was able to create this wonderful potato pancake. Great for brunch, lunch, or even a light dinner.

Peel the potatoes and grate them as if for hash browns. Divide into two portions. Separate the salmon into small pieces no bigger than ½ inch, and divide. In a 10-inch nonstick skillet melt 1 tablespoon of butter over medium high heat and swirl until the entire bottom is coated. Add the first portion of potatoes to the pan, spreading in an even layer. Working quickly, distribute the salmon pieces over the pancake, and press them down into the potatoes. Sprinkle with half of the paprika and salt to taste. When the first side is brown (about 5 minutes), turn the pancake over using two spatulas, or by flipping it if you are skilled at that. Cover the pan and allow to cook for 4 to 5 more minutes. Remove to a serving platter and repeat with the second pancake. Keep the serving platter in the oven until the second pancake is done. Makes 8 servings.

French Red Potato Salad

This is another favorite from my catering business. I was very concerned about serving salads with a mayonnaise base for events that were held outdoors in hot weather. This potato salad was the perfect solution because it had a vinegar, wine, and oil dressing, and actually tastes better when it's warm. Try it for your next picnic.

2	pounds red potatoes
8	green onions, sliced thin
2	tablespoons Italian parsley, minced
1	teaspoon dill weed
½	teaspoon salt
¼	teaspoon cracked pepper
3	tablespoons rice vinegar
¼	cup white wine
2	teaspoons minced garlic
½	cup olive oil

Cut the potatoes into quarters, and steam for 15 minutes or until cooked through but not mushy. Drain in a colander and rinse in cold water. When cool enough to handle, cut the potatoes into cubes and transfer to a large mixing bowl. Add the onions, parsley, dill weed, salt, and pepper, and stir to distribute. In a small bowl whisk together the vinegar, wine, garlic, and olive oil. Pour over the potatoes and stir thoroughly. Serve immediately or chill and serve later. Makes 8 servings.

Potatoes are high in starch but also high in fiber. When potatoes are cooked and then mashed and puréed, they will add a natural creaminess to dishes like soup or stew. The fiber in potatoes keeps them in one piece when they're diced and added to soups or other vegetable dishes, or when cooked and chilled for salad. When cooked, they can be a little bland, so they need lots of seasoning, such as pungent herbs, salt or salty foods, onion, garlic, pepper, or wine. Potatoes can be baked or roasted with other vegetables, and added to meat, poultry, or fish stews. They are tasty when roasted or cooked by themselves, with a light seasoning of some kind. Mashed potatoes can be used as a casserole base or topping, or also added to yeast breads.

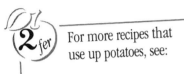

For more recipes that use up potatoes, see:

Potato Gratin, p. 54
Scalloped Parsley Potatoes, p. 101
Bouillabaisse, p. 191

NOTES

_____
_____
_____
_____
_____
_____
_____
_____
_____
_____

From the kitchen of ⎯⎯⎯⎯⎯⎯⎯⎯⎯

From the kitchen of ⎯⎯⎯⎯⎯⎯⎯⎯⎯

19
Raisins

Raisins come in little tiny lunch-box-size boxes or big boxes where they end up sticking together in the corners, or you can even buy them in bulk, where they stick together in the corner of the bin. Raisins are really dried grapes; Thompson seedless or Red Flame grapes are used for most of the commercial raisins. As such, they have a natural tart sweetness. Raisins keep for a relatively long time, but can become dried out, or can get mushy and stick to other raisins in the package. Raisins add a subtle sweet flavor to lots of different foods, and once you try some of the recipes in this chapter, you may never eat plain raisins again!

Raisin Toasting Bread

This is a wonderful bread with a fine crumb, yet sturdy enough to be toasted and buttered. Because you roll the raisins inside the loaf, none of them become charred, as they would if you mixed them within the batter. The cinnamon in the batter and also in the swirl complements the raisins nicely. This makes a nice tall loaf.

2	teaspoons instant yeast
2	teaspoons cinnamon
½	teaspoon salt
3	tablespoons sugar
4	cups (approximately) all-purpose flour
1	cup warm water at "bread" temperature (105°)
¼	cup melted butter
1	egg
	Melted butter for brushing
1	tablespoon sugar
½	teaspoon cinnamon
¾	cup raisins

In a large mixing bowl blend the yeast, cinnamon, salt, sugar, and 2 cups flour. Mix until blended. Test the water temperature with a thermometer. Add to the mixing bowl along with ¼ cup melted butter. Mix again, then add the egg and mix until thoroughly blended. Add enough remaining flour until the dough clings together and leaves the side of the mixing bowl. Transfer to a floured board; knead until smooth and elastic. Allow to rise until doubled, at least 45 minutes.

Preheat the oven to 375°. Spray a 5 x 9-inch loaf pan with a light coating of cooking spray. Place the dough on a floured board and punch down, then roll it out so that it is the width of the loaf pan and about 12 inches long. Brush the surface of the dough with melted butter. In a small bowl mix together 1 tablespoon sugar and ½ teaspoon cinnamon, and sprinkle evenly over the dough. Sprinkle the raisins over the dough. Roll up tightly and seal the seam. Place seam side down in the prepared loaf pan. Allow to rise for about 20 minutes, until almost double. To avoid over-browning the bottom, cook on the center rack. Bake for 35 to 40 minutes or until browned. Makes 1 loaf.

1   cup dried fruit such as
    apricots, peaches,
    plums, or cherries
½   cup raisins
1   tablespoon butter
2   apples or pears, peeled
    and sliced
2   oranges, peeled and cut
    into sections
½   teaspoon cinnamon
2   tablespoons brown
    sugar
2   tablespoons brandy

Winter Fruit Compote

A compote is usually a mixture of fruit stewed together in liquid. Sounds rather bland, doesn't it? This recipe takes compote to a new level, spicing it up with cinnamon and brandy. The result is a rich and flavorful mixture that is wonderful served with a little vanilla ice cream, or it can be spooned over waffles or pancakes.

Soften the dried fruit and raisins by placing them in a bowl with enough hot water to cover. Let sit for 30 minutes.

In a large skillet melt the butter and add the apples or pears. Sauté for 2 minutes, until soft. Add the orange sections and sauté for 1 more minute. Drain the dried fruit in a colander and add to the skillet. Stir to mix the fruit together. Sprinkle the cinnamon and brown sugar over the top and cook for 3 more minutes over medium heat. Add the brandy and cook for 2 more minutes. Serve warm. Makes 8 servings.

Spinach Raisin Sauté

If you want a nutritious vegetable dish loaded with iron, try combining spinach with raisins! In addition to being a healthful duo, they taste wonderful together and look festive. This is a great side dish to serve with fish or grilled meats.

2 teaspoons olive oil
1 teaspoon minced garlic
2 tablespoons pine nuts
10 ounces fresh spinach
½ cup raisins
2 tablespoons water

In a large skillet heat the olive oil and brown the garlic and pine nuts. Remove from the pan and set aside. Add the spinach to the pan and brown slightly. Add the raisins and water, cover, and let cook over medium heat for about 5 minutes, until the spinach is cooked. Return the garlic and pine nuts to the pan and stir. Makes 4 servings.

1   cup brown rice
2½   cups water
½   cup pine nuts
1   tablespoon olive oil
¼   cup chopped onion
¾   cup raisins
2   tablespoons water
3   tablespoons chopped
     fresh mint leaves

Exotic Pilaf

The flavors of mint, raisins, and pine nuts liven up this brown rice dish. Usually a pilaf is made in one step; in this recipe the rice is cooked separately first and then sautéed with the other ingredients.

In a medium saucepan cook the brown rice in the water over medium heat until done, about 40 minutes. Remove from the heat, stir, and keep warm.

On a baking sheet toast the pine nuts in a 350° oven for 8 minutes; set aside. In a large skillet heat the olive oil and brown the onion until golden. Add the raisins, and sauté for 2 minutes. Add the brown rice to the pan, and stir to distribute the onions and raisins. Add 2 table-spoons water to prevent the rice from sticking to the pan. When the rice is heated through, stir in the mint and pine nuts, and then serve. Makes 6 to 8 servings.

Brandy Apple Crisp

I make all types of fruit crisps year-round, but this one made with apples in the fall is my favorite. The brandy gives an extra zing to the raisins and the apples.

1 cup raisins
3 tablespoons brandy
5 cups peeled and sliced apples (Braeburn, Rome, or Gala)
1 tablespoon lemon juice
1 teaspoon cinnamon
¼ cup brown sugar

Topping:
¼ cup all-purpose flour
¼ cup butter
½ cup brown sugar
½ teaspoon cinnamon
1½ cups rolled oats

In a small bowl soak the raisins in brandy for about 30 minutes. Preheat the oven to 350°. Spray a 9 x 13-inch pan with cooking spray. Place the apple slices in the prepared pan. Sprinkle with lemon juice, cinnamon, and brown sugar, and stir to coat evenly. Add the raisin-brandy mixture to the pan and stir to distribute.

To make the topping, in a food processor or blender place the flour, butter, brown sugar, and cinnamon and mix until crumbly. Add the rolled oats and mix again until the oats are distributed but not grainy. Sprinkle the topping over the apple-raisin mixture in the pan. Bake for 45 minutes. Makes 8 to 12 servings.

When you use raisins in other recipes, you may need to add moisture back into the raisins by soaking them in water or some other liquid, which results in a juicier raisin. The exception might be baked goods such as breads, muffins, cookies, or scones, where the raisins are already the right consistency. Raisins add a distinct tartness to sweet baked goods as well as a chewy texture. They go well with almost any type of nuts in baked goods, but particularly walnuts. Raisins can be added to meat or chicken dishes in a sauce that has some tart ingredients in it such as tomatoes or wine; the raisins will tone down the tartness in the dish. Raisins blend well with most other fruits in fruit salads or cooked fruit dishes such as cobblers.

NOTES

From the kitchen of —————

From the kitchen of —————

20
Rice (Cooked)

White or brown rice is a popular side dish, easily used as a base for Asian food, sauces, or stews. When it's served in a separate bowl, it seems there's always some left over. Cooked rice that's stored in the refrigerator tends to dry out very easily and doesn't reheat well unless rehydrated somehow, and even then it often tastes stale. When you reuse rice in a dish and add liquids or moist ingredients, however, the rice regains its original consistency. These recipes use cooked rice to add body, texture, or as a base to introduce new flavors to a dish. These recipes were developed for white rice, but brown rice works equally well and lends a nuttier flavor.

Sun-Rice Eggs

When I was growing up, my father had to follow a bland diet. For breakfast, my mother would make him scrambled eggs in a double boiler because he couldn't eat anything fried. For variety, she added some cooked white rice to the eggs. After I tasted them, I always asked her to make another serving for me. Over time, I've adapted the recipe to suit my evolving tastes (and I don't have to use a double boiler).

1	tablespoon butter or olive oil
1	cup cooked rice
¼	teaspoon dill weed
⅛	teaspoon salt
⅛	teaspoon pepper
4	whole eggs, beaten

Heat a nonstick sauté pan over medium high heat. Add the butter or oil and swirl to coat the bottom of the pan. Add the rice to the pan, and sprinkle the dill weed, salt, and pepper over the rice. Stir and sauté for 2 minutes. Add the beaten eggs to the pan, and stir until the eggs are cooked through. Makes 4 servings.

2 fer
Also uses eggs

1   tablespoon fruity olive oil
1   clove garlic, minced
3   brown or white mushrooms, sliced thin
2   tablespoons chopped fresh basil or
    ½ teaspoon dried
1   cup fresh spinach or chard, sliced in strips
2   tablespoons pine nuts
1   cup cooked white rice
1   egg white
    Salt and pepper to taste

Risotto Fritto

Take a Chinese cooking technique and combine it with Italian flavors for Italian Fried Rice! This is a versatile dish, and you can add different vegetables or herbs depending on what you have on hand. Risotto Fritto makes a great side dish to serve with Italian sausage or fish.

In a large sauté pan heat the olive oil and add the garlic, mushrooms, and half of the basil. Sauté until the mushrooms are lightly browned. Add the spinach or chard and pine nuts; stir-fry for 2 minutes. Add the rice and sauté until heated through. Add the egg white and stir thoroughly. Stir in the remaining basil. Cook until the mixture sticks together. Add salt and pepper to taste, then serve. Makes 4 servings.

Luau Pudding

The tropical flavor of coconut and pineapple provide a refreshing lift to cooked rice. Serve chilled when the pudding is set.

1 0.8-ounce box cook 'n' serve vanilla pudding mix (not instant)
1½ cups milk
1 8-ounce can pineapple chunks, drained
1 cup cold cooked rice
2 tablespoons unsweetened shredded coconut
½ teaspoon coconut extract

In a saucepan prepare the pudding with the milk according to package directions. Let cool for 5 minutes. In a large mixing bowl stir together the pineapple, rice, coconut, and coconut extract. Pour the cooled pudding over this mixture and blend well. Pour into a glass bowl or casserole dish and refrigerate until the pudding is set. Makes 4 servings.

Also uses milk

6   green cabbage leaves
½   cup sauerkraut
1   8-ounce can tomato
     sauce
½   pound ground turkey
1½   cups cold cooked rice
2   tablespoons minced
     shallots
     Salt and pepper to taste

Pigs in the Blanket

This is another recipe from my childhood that I've adapted through the years. My mother would always use ground beef to make these cabbage rolls, but I've since lightened them a little with ground turkey.

Preheat the oven to 350°. Blanch the cabbage leaves in boiling water for 5 minutes. Remove the leaves, rinse in a colander and let cool. In a 1½- to 2-quart ovenproof casserole, evenly spread ¼ cup of the sauerkraut across the bottom. Spread 2 tablespoons of the tomato sauce over the sauerkraut layer. In a large mixing bowl stir together the ground turkey, rice, shallots, salt, and pepper. Reserve 2 tablespoons of the tomato sauce and set aside; add the remainder of the tomato sauce to the bowl. Blend well, then divide the mixture into 6 portions. Place each portion of filling on a cabbage leaf and fold the sides of the leaf over, sealing the roll. Place each roll seam side down in the casserole. Place a dab of sauerkraut on top of each roll, then a dab of tomato sauce. Bake for 45 minutes. Makes 6 servings.

Stuffed Peppers

This is a light version of stuffed peppers made with ground turkey. You can also use ground beef if you prefer. The pine nuts and capers add extra crunch to the filling.

Preheat the oven to 350°. On a baking sheet toast the pine nuts in the oven for 8 minutes. Set aside. Spray a tall casserole dish large enough to hold the peppers with cooking spray. Cut a small horizontal slice off the top of each pepper and scoop out the seeds. Rinse the peppers inside and out. Place in the prepared casserole. To make the filling, in a large bowl mix together the ground turkey, rice, tomato sauce, capers, garlic, basil, parsley, and toasted pine nuts. Stuff the mixture into the peppers. Pour about ½ cup of water around the peppers in the casserole. Bake, covered, for 30 minutes. Makes 4 servings.

¼ cup pine nuts
4 bell peppers
1 pound ground turkey
2 cups cooked rice
1 8-ounce can tomato sauce
1 tablespoon capers
1 tablespoon minced garlic
2 tablespoons chopped fresh basil
2 tablespoons chopped parsley

Rice is a starch and has a tendency to absorb flavors pretty easily. Because rice by itself is rather bland, you'll want to add herbs and spices or flavors that are salty, tart, or pungent when you cook with it the second time around. Tart flavors, such as citrus, apricot, or tomato, work well with rice, and so do pungent seasonings and ingredients like wine, peppers, or vinegar. Salty ingredients, such as soy sauce or smoked meats, add interest as well. Sweet foods can work with rice, but there should be at least one tart ingredient, such as adding raisins or tart fruit to rice pudding.

You'll also need to add a lot of liquid or wet ingredients when you work with cooked rice. Unlike other starches, rice retains its texture after it's cooked. When it is reintroduced to a dish, rice can create an interesting contrast in texture, such as adding rice to a smooth dish such as scrambled eggs. Think crunchy and smooth together to create contrast.

2 fer For more recipes that use up rice, see:

Confetti Carrot Bake, p. 36

NOTES

_____

_____

_____

_____

_____

_____

_____

_____

From the kitchen of ———

From the kitchen of ———

21
Salad Dressing

Why is it that in the average family, no two people like the same type of dressing on their salads? Sometimes people are on a diet and want a dressing with less or no fat. Sometimes you'll have a bottle of some gourmet dressing you bought for a dinner party and you haven't used it since. Most bottled dressings will last a fairly long time in the refrigerator, but if you deeply desire to free up some space in the refrigerator, maybe it's time to retire some of the salad dressing by cooking with it. Most bottled dressings come in 12-ounce or 16-ounce bottles, but once again, a little goes a long way and most of the time only a few tablespoons are used on the average salad. These recipes use a little more than that, and before you know it, you have more room in the refrigerator. Note that these recipes are designed for oil and vinegar dressings such as Italian, French, or Caesar, but not for creamy dressings.

Sassy Chicken

One of the great things about salad dressing is that it contains some oil, which is good for cooking things; and some lemon or vinegar, which is good for tenderizing things. The combination provides a wonderful and fast way to cook chicken in a skillet. I've used chicken thighs in this recipe, but it can also be made with breasts, legs, or any bone-in chicken pieces.

6	chicken thighs, skin removed
⅛	teaspoon each paprika and salt, combined
1	tablespoon olive oil
¼	cup chopped onion
½	cup mixture of salad dressing and chicken broth, using up to ¼ cup salad dressing Chopped parsley for garnish

Sprinkle the chicken with the paprika-salt mixture. In a skillet with a tight-fitting lid heat the olive oil and brown the onion lightly over medium high heat. Add the chicken and brown on both sides. In a measuring cup combine the salad dressing and chicken broth so that you have ½ cup of liquid. Pour over the chicken. Cover and reduce the heat to medium. Cook for 15 minutes, turn the chicken and cook for 10 more minutes, or until done. Sprinkle with parsley to serve. Makes 6 servings.

2   cups cooked brown and
    wild rice mix
1   cup diced cucumber,
    peel on
½   cup diced radishes
2   green onions, thinly
    sliced
10 cherry tomatoes, cut
    into quarters
2   tablespoons chopped
    parsley
2   tablespoons olive oil
1   tablespoon lemon juice
½   cup bottled salad
    dressing

Veggie Rice Salad

The next time you go to make potato salad, try this rice salad instead for a refreshing change. The crisp and colorful vegetables and the crunchiness of the wild and brown rice are a wonderful combination. Serve it at your next barbecue.

In a medium bowl combine the rice, cucumber, radishes, onions, tomatoes, and parsley. Stir well. Break up any clumps of rice to make sure the grains are separate. In a smaller bowl whisk together the olive oil, lemon juice, and salad dressing. Pour over the rice mixture, and stir thoroughly. Refrigerate for at least 4 hours or overnight to blend flavors. Makes 8 servings.

Jazzed-Up Couscous

Couscous is a nice alternative to rice or potatoes. It is a form of pasta, although it is so tiny, you'd never guess it. Packaged plain, couscous is usually prepared with just water and a little bit of butter, but that can be very bland. Salad dressing added to the cooking water really perks it up, along with the sautéed mushrooms. This is a wonderful side dish for meat, poultry, or fish.

Up to ¼ cup salad dressing

1   cup couscous
1   teaspoon olive oil
4   mushrooms, diced
2   tablespoons chopped parsley

In a measuring cup combine the salad dressing with water to equal 1 cup of liquid. Place in a saucepan and bring to a boil. Add the couscous and let it come to a boil again. Remove from the heat and let sit for 5 minutes, covered. Meanwhile, in a skillet heat the olive oil and sauté the mushrooms and parsley. Add to the couscous and stir, breaking up any clumps. Makes 4 servings.

1   pound fresh broccoli
8   ounces fresh
    mushrooms, sliced
8   green onions, sliced thin
Dressing:
½   cup salad dressing
2   tablespoons rice vinegar
¼   cup olive oil
1   teaspoon paprika
1   teaspoon onion powder
¼   cup sugar
½   teaspoon salt

Broccoli Salad

Most people wouldn't think of using broccoli in a marinated salad, but this has a wonderful flavor. Great for a potluck, and a wonderful alternative to tossed salad.

Cut the broccoli into small flowerets or 1-inch pieces. Place in a large mixing bowl along with the mushrooms and green onions. In a small bowl whisk together the ingredients for the dressing, and toss with the broccoli mixture. Refrigerate for at least 1 hour before serving. Makes 6 to 8 servings.

Picnic Loaf

There are many variations of this recipe; some use chicken or turkey, some use tuna. Whatever the filling, leftover salad dressing is perfect for this recipe.

1	long loaf of sourdough or crusty bread
1	can tuna, drained
½	cup radishes, diced
½	cup cucumbers, peeled and diced
4	Roma tomatoes, diced
1	tablespoon capers
4	green onions, sliced
½	teaspoon dried basil
½	teaspoon minced garlic
¼	cup salad dressing

Slice the bread loaf horizontally and remove the top. Scoop out some of the bread on the bottom part to create a hollow for the filling. Crumble about 1 cup of the bread pieces and place in a large mixing bowl. Add the tuna, radishes, cucumbers, tomatoes, capers, green onions, basil, garlic, and salad dressing, and stir until well blended. Spread the mixture into the hollow of the bread. Place the top of the loaf back on and wrap tightly in foil. Let sit at room temperature right side up for one hour, then invert it so that it's upside down for 1 hour (this will flavor the top of the bread). Slice crosswise to serve. Makes 8 servings.

When you're using salad dressing in another dish, remember that it already has a certain amount of oil and vinegar in it. In order to use the dressing in another dish that will be cooked, you will need to add more liquid to it. That will dilute the flavor a little bit. If you're using salad dressing as part of a marinade and you have a small amount to use up, you will need to add more oil and vinegar or other liquid to it in order to make enough to cover the food you're marinating. Sometimes you can use the dressing as is in a recipe and you don't need to add anything else to it, such as using it for other types of salads such as potato or cooked vegetable salads. Keep in mind that salad dressing also has a lot of seasonings and salt in it already, so use a light touch when adding herbs to a dish. Salad dressing can be added to baked goods such as yeast breads, in place of butter or oil or as part of the liquid. It will add moisture and extra flavor to the bread.

NOTES

From the kitchen of

From the kitchen of

22
Salsa

Once a little-known condiment in most of the United States, salsa has nearly replaced catsup in today's kitchen. The most common use of salsa is of course as an accompaniment to tortilla chips, but when the chips are gone there always seems to be some of that salsa left in the container. Salsas are marketed in two forms: fresh-cut, which is refrigerated, and cooked, sold in jars or cans. Fresh-cut salsa is tangier, with crispy chunks of tomato, chili, and onion, whereas cooked salsa is more sauce-like in texture. Either type works well in the following recipes. Salsa consists of a wonderful mixture of pungent flavors including onion, cilantro, chili peppers, tomato, lime, and sometimes garlic. When you add this mixture to other recipes such as those that follow, all the individual flavors carry over to the new creation.

Spanish Rice

The traditional recipe for Spanish Rice involves adding a bit of tomato juice or paste, and a little "heat" such as chili powder or cayenne. But why not use salsa instead with all of its wonderful individual flavors like onion, cilantro, tomato and lime? Rice works like a charm to absorb and showcase all those flavors, and this makes a great side dish for meats, poultry, or barbecue.

1 tablespoon olive oil
½ cup chopped onion
1 cup uncooked long-grain white rice
1½ cups water
1 cup salsa
½ teaspoon salt

In a large saucepan or braising pan heat the olive oil and sauté the onion over medium high heat. Add the rice and sauté for 2 or 3 more minutes, until the rice is opaque but not browned. Stand back, then pour the water and salsa into the pan (it may sizzle and spatter). Add the salt. Reduce the heat to low, cover, and simmer for 10 minutes. Uncover and stir once all the way through. If it looks dry, add a bit more water. Cover and simmer for 10 more minutes. Makes 8 servings.

Meatballs:

¼ pound ground turkey or beef

¼ teaspoon cumin

¼ teaspoon oregano

¼ teaspoon onion powder

⅛ teaspoon chili powder

Soup:

5 cups chicken broth

½ cup sliced green onions, including tops

1 yellow 2-inch hot chili pepper (Anaheim)

1 cup chopped unpeeled fresh tomatoes

½ cup salsa

2 tablespoons fresh cilantro, minced

4 zucchini squash, diced

½ cup corn cut from cob, or frozen corn kernels

Baja Soup

The flavors in salsa are terrific for soup. This hearty soup has meatballs and vegetables added to the colorful and spicy broth. Serve with fresh tortillas for a festive and flavorful one-pot meal.

For the meatballs, preheat the oven to 500°. Line a shallow pan with aluminum foil. Mix the turkey or beef with the spices and blend thoroughly. Shape into 12 meatballs. Bake in the prepared pan for 25 minutes. Allow to cool.

For the soup, bring the broth to a boil in a soup pot. Add the green onions and simmer for 10 minutes. Mince the chili pepper and add to the soup along with the tomatoes, salsa, and cilantro. Simmer for 15 minutes, then add the squash and corn, and simmer for 10 more minutes, or until the squash is cooked through. Add the meatballs to the soup just before serving, and garnish with additional fresh cilantro. Makes 4 main-dish servings.

Also uses tomatoes

Mexicali Meatloaf

Classic meatloaf recipes can sometimes be bland. Try adding salsa to liven it up a little. The crunch from the salsa adds texture, and the flavors blend well with the cornmeal that is used to thicken and shape the meatloaf. Olé!

1	teaspoon olive oil
½	cup diced onion
1	pound ground turkey, beef, or combination
⅓	cup cornmeal
1	egg
½	teaspoon cumin
¾	cup salsa
¼	teaspoon salt

Preheat the oven to 350°. In a saucepan heat the olive oil and sauté the onion until golden. Set aside. In a large mixing bowl blend the ground meat with the cornmeal, egg, cumin, ½ cup salsa, and salt until thoroughly blended. Stir in the cooked onion and blend well. Pour into a 4 x 8-inch loaf pan and smooth the top. Spoon ¼ cup salsa over the top. Bake for 1 hour. Chill the leftovers and slice for great meatloaf sandwiches. Makes 8 to 12 servings.

1   pound summer squash,
    any type
1   tablespoon olive oil
2   cloves garlic, minced
½   cup salsa

Salsa Summer Squash

Summer squash, such as zucchini, crookneck, or pattypan, is a very versatile vegetable, but unfortunately it is rather bland by itself. Salsa wakes up the flavor of the squash in this speedy recipe. You can also serve this dish cold as a salad; just add a dash of rice vinegar. For those of you who grow squash in your garden, this is a great way to use the often overabundant harvest as well.

Depending on the size and shape of the squash, slice or dice it into 1-inch pieces. In a large skillet heat the olive oil over medium high heat. Sauté the garlic for 1 minute, then add the squash and sauté for about 5 minutes until slightly browned. Reduce the heat to medium, and add the salsa. Stir and then cover. Cook for about 10 minutes, checking to make sure the squash does not dry out—add 1 to 2 tablespoons of water if it does. After 10 minutes, check to make sure the squash is cooked through. Do not overcook. Makes 4 servings.

Black Bean Salad

This is a very colorful salad, and makes a festive dish to serve at a barbecue or for a potluck. It's also a great main-dish salad; just serve with warm tortillas.

1	15-ounce can black beans
1	8¾-ounce can kernel corn
1	cup salsa
2	tablespoons olive oil
1	teaspoon sugar (approximately)
¼	cup diced celery
½	cup diced avocado
	Fresh cilantro for garnish

In a colander drain the beans and corn. In a large mixing bowl place the salsa and add the olive oil and sugar. Stir together, then taste. Depending on the tartness of the salsa, you may want to add a little more sugar or a little salt. Add the beans, corn, and celery to the salsa mixture, and toss to distribute evenly. Stir in the avocado gently so that the pieces keep their shape. Refrigerate. Garnish with fresh cilantro before serving. Makes 8 servings.

The pungency of salsa can add interest to otherwise bland ingredients. Adding it to meats, starches such as rice or potatoes, or starchy vegetables will result in a wonderful contrast. Fresh-cut salsa should be used within a week of purchase. Cooked salsa may keep a bit longer in the refrigerator. Think of the ingredients in salsa as a set of individual spices and flavors that are already mixed together, which can be added to other sauces, soups, casseroles, or even salad dressings. You can put salsa in a blender to make a gazpacho-type soup base to add other vegetables. You can also use it as a topping for pizza—sprinkle it with cheese, and there you have it: Mexican pizza.

NOTES

_____

_____

_____

_____

_____

_____

_____

_____

_____

_____

_____

_____

From the kitchen of ——————————

From the kitchen of ——————————

23
Tomato Paste

Why is it that so many recipes call for just a tablespoon of tomato paste? That makes me crazy. I must have thrown away the remainders of a hundred cans of tomato paste in my cooking lifetime until I started being creative with it. In fact, this one ingredient is what drove me to write this book to begin with. Tomato paste is very thick and concentrated; I don't know how many tomatoes it takes to make a six-ounce can of the stuff, but there must be about a thousand of them in there. It's so sticky that sometimes I have to use a knife as a little spatula to pry it out of the can. Because it is so concentrated, it takes just a little to thicken an entire recipe of pasta sauce. So, I've developed recipes that use the rest of the can, and, as you can imagine, these recipes have lots of tomato flavor in them.

Cha Cha Chili

This chili will make you light on your feet! Made with ground turkey, it is lower in fat than most chili recipes. If you want your chili hotter, you can add more chili powder, or add a small 4-ounce can of chopped green chilies to the recipe. Olé!

In a sauté pan heat the olive oil and brown the turkey, onion, garlic, and cumin over medium high heat until the turkey is no longer pink. Transfer to a soup pot or large Dutch oven. Add the tomatoes, tomato paste, water, beans, chili powder, and salt. Bring to a boil, and then reduce the heat to medium low. Simmer for 45 minutes. Makes 6 servings.

2	teaspoons olive oil
½	pound ground turkey
1	medium onion, chopped
3	small cloves garlic, minced
½	teaspoon ground cumin
1	28-ounce can chopped tomatoes (or 4 cups fresh)
¾	6-ounce can tomato paste, or whatever you have left
2	cups water
1	15-ounce can pinto beans, drained and rinsed
1	15-ounce can kidney beans, drained and rinsed
1	tablespoon chili powder
1	teaspoon salt

Also uses onions
and tomatoes

1   tablespoon olive oil
½   onion, finely chopped
¼   cup finely chopped
    celery
½   pound ground turkey
¾   6-ounce can tomato
    paste
2   tablespoons catsup
2   tablespoons pickle relish
1   teaspoon paprika
1   teaspoon salt
1   cup water

Sloppy Toms

I decided to try making Sloppy Joes with ground turkey, for a change. Because ground turkey doesn't have as much fat, it's hard to get a smooth consistency that blends with the sauce. And Sloppy Joes have to be messy! Grinding the cooked turkey does the trick.

In a sauté pan heat the olive oil and sauté the onion and celery. Add the turkey and brown. Transfer the mixture to a blender or food processor and process until smooth and no lumpy pieces remain. Return the mixture to the sauté pan. Add the tomato paste, catsup, relish, paprika, salt, and water, and cook over low heat for 15 minutes. Add more water if necessary for a "sloppy" consistency. Spoon onto hamburger buns and serve. Makes 6 servings.

Red Velvet Snapper

Tomato paste lends a velvety texture to foods; hence the name of this recipe. However, it also can be rather heavy, and the lemon juice lightens up this sauce a bit. The almonds add a little crunch to give it some texture.

Preheat the oven to 400°. Spray a shallow glass baking pan with cooking spray. Cut the fish into serving-sized pieces. In a large skillet heat the olive oil and sauté the fish over medium high heat for 1 to 2 minutes on each side. Place in the prepared pan. In the same skillet sauté the onions and garlic briefly, then add the tomato paste, broth, almonds, lemon rind, lemon juice, and basil, and stir until the sauce is well blended. Spoon over the fish fillets. Bake for 15 minutes (don't overbake or the fish will dry out). Sprinkle with a little chopped parsley to serve. Makes 3 to 4 servings.

1	pound red snapper fillets
2	teaspoons olive oil
¼	cup minced onion
1	teaspoon minced garlic
¼	cup tomato paste
¼	cup chicken broth
2	tablespoons finely chopped almonds
	Grated rind of 1 lemon
2	teaspoons lemon juice
¼	teaspoon basil
	Chopped parsley for garnish

½   cup (1 stick) butter
½   cup granulated sugar
¼   cup brown sugar
2   eggs
¼   cup tomato paste
1   8-ounce carton vanilla
    yogurt
1   cup apple juice
1¾ cups all-purpose flour
¾   cup rolled oats
1   teaspoon baking soda
1   tablespoon baking
    powder
½   teaspoon cinnamon
½   teaspoon salt
½   cup diced dates
1   cup pecan pieces

Sunset Pecan Bread

People will never guess that this bread has tomato paste in it. Not only does it give the bread a sweet, moist texture, but it also turns it a beautiful sunset color.

Preheat the oven to 350°. Spray a 5 x 9-inch loaf pan with cooking spray. In a large bowl cream the butter and sugars using an electric mixer. Add the eggs, tomato paste, yogurt, and half of the apple juice. Mix until smooth. In a smaller bowl blend the flour, oats, soda, baking powder, cinnamon, and salt. Add to the butter mixture and stir until very smooth. Add the remaining apple juice, dates, and pecans, and blend to distribute. Bake for 1 hour. Makes 12 servings.

Tri-Tomato Soup

Tomato lovers, this is the soup for you. It uses fresh tomatoes, tomato paste, and some sun-dried tomatoes, all of which contribute their own unique flavors to the soup. This is also a very low-calorie but filling soup.

In a large soup pot heat 1 teaspoon olive oil and sauté the onion, garlic, and celery for 2 to 3 minutes. Add the basil and oregano and stir. Add 1 more teaspoon of olive oil to the pan, then add the rice and sauté for 3 to 4 minutes until the rice is opaque. Add the chopped fresh tomatoes, sun-dried tomatoes, and broth. Bring to a boil and simmer for 20 minutes. Meanwhile, in a medium skillet heat 1 teaspoon olive oil and sauté the zucchini and mushrooms for 3 minutes; set aside. Add the tomato paste and water to the stock pot and simmer for 10 more minutes. Add the zucchini, mushrooms, and spinach, and simmer for 10 more minutes or until all of the vegetables are cooked through. Add salt and pepper to taste. Makes 4 to 6 servings.

1 tablespoon olive oil, divided
½ cup chopped onion
2 cloves garlic, minced
2 stalks celery, chopped
½ teaspoon dried basil
¼ teaspoon dried oregano
¼ cup uncooked rice (white or brown)
2 medium tomatoes, chopped
2 tablespoons sun-dried tomatoes, chopped into ¼-inch pieces
2 cups chicken broth
1 zucchini, cut into matchsticks
¾ cup sliced mushrooms
¾ 6-ounce can tomato paste
3½ cups water
1 cup spinach or chard leaves
Salt and pepper to taste

The objective here is to use up the rest of the can of this concentrated tomato flavor, so think lots of liquid and lots of volume. That's why adding tomato paste to soups is a wonderful solution because you add lots of liquid and the soup won't be bland. Tomato paste makes a great base for sauces that can be used with poultry, fish, or meats; it thickens the sauce and makes it easy to coat whatever you're cooking. The flavor of tomato paste is sweet and has a pungent tomato flavor, so to balance it out, you will need more acidic or tart flavors such as wine, vinegar, soy sauce, hot peppers, or garlic. Because it is sweet, tomato paste can be an unusual ingredient in yeast breads, but bear in mind that it will also add a lot of color to the bread as well.

NOTES

From the kitchen of ⎯⎯⎯⎯⎯⎯⎯⎯⎯⎯⎯⎯⎯⎯⎯⎯

From the kitchen of ⎯⎯⎯⎯⎯⎯⎯⎯⎯⎯⎯⎯⎯⎯⎯⎯

24

Tomatoes

Such a versatile food. Tomatoes are delicate, juicy, flavorful, and mouthwatering when they are picked at the peak of ripeness. They come in all sizes and shapes, and, more recently, they even come in other colors such as yellow or green. Tomatoes are at their best in the summertime and if you're lucky enough to have some growing in your garden, chances are you will be eating them nearly every day. When you need more ideas for using up an over-abundant harvest, turn to this chapter. In the wintertime, it's harder to find good tomatoes, and they just don't have as much flavor. Stored in the refrigerator, they can sometimes lose even more flavor. Before tomatoes start getting mushy and when they're starting to get ugly, it's time to use them up in other dishes.

Flash Minestrone

Ever look at a minestrone recipe and think, "There are too many steps and there's too little time!" Well, this one is fast and can be ready in just one hour.

In a soup pot, combine the tomatoes, onion, carrot, garlic, oregano, thyme, basil, salt, and water. Bring to a boil, then reduce the heat and simmer for 30 minutes while you're getting the rest of the ingredients ready. Add the tomato juice, beans, chard, zucchini, and cauliflower. Simmer for 15 minutes covered, then 15 minutes uncovered. Add more salt to taste if desired. Makes 6 to 8 servings.

4	ugly tomatoes
1	cup chopped onion
1	carrot, diced
2	cloves garlic, minced
1	teaspoon dried oregano
½	teaspoon thyme
1	teaspoon dried basil
½	teaspoon salt
1	quart water
1	11.5-ounce can tomato juice
1	15-ounce can cannellini or kidney beans, drained
½	bunch chard, sliced
2	zucchini, sliced
1	cup cauliflower, cut into small pieces

Also uses onions

1   teaspoon olive oil
6   loin pork chops
1   cup chopped onion
½   cup chopped celery
4   ugly tomatoes
1   8-ounce can tomato
    sauce
2   teaspoons
    Worcestershire sauce
2   teaspoons sugar
½   teaspoon dried thyme
    Salt and pepper to taste

Saucy Oven Pork Chops

These pork chops are very tasty and tender. The acid in tomatoes has a tenderizing effect on most meats, especially when baked in the oven.

Preheat the oven to 350°. In a large skillet heat the olive oil and brown the pork chops on both sides over medium high heat. Transfer to a covered casserole (you can layer the pork chops one on top of the other for this recipe). In the same skillet place the onion and celery and brown briefly. Add the tomatoes and cook for 5 minutes, until the tomatoes are soft. Add the tomato sauce, Worcestershire, sugar, and thyme to the pan, along with a little salt and pepper. Cook for about 5 more minutes, then pour over the pork chops. Bake, covered, for 45 minutes. Makes 6 servings.

Also uses onions

Leek-Tomato Risotto

Most risotto recipes are made on the stovetop and require a lot of attention. With this one, you can put it in the oven and ignore it. The tomatoes provide additional moisture for the dish and add a wonderful flavor.

¼ cup olive oil

2 leeks, cleaned and thinly sliced

3 ugly tomatoes

½ teaspoon thyme

½ teaspoon salt

⅛ teaspoon white pepper

1½ cups arborio (risotto) rice

3½ cups chicken broth

2 tablespoons chopped Italian parsley

Preheat the oven to 350°. Brush a covered 2-quart casserole with olive oil. In a large skillet heat the olive oil and brown the leeks for 2 minutes. Add the tomatoes, thyme, salt, and pepper. Stir until the tomatoes become soft. Add the rice and stir briefly, then transfer the mixture to the prepared casserole. Pour the broth over, then stir. Bake for 30 to 45 minutes, checking to see if the rice is soft. When done, stir the rice to fluff and add the chopped parsley. Makes 8 servings.

6	Roma tomatoes
2	tablespoons olive oil
1	teaspoon garlic
	Salt to taste
	Cracked pepper
¼	cup fresh basil, chopped

Instant Pasta Sauce

This recipe works best with Roma tomatoes, but you can also use other types of tomatoes that are not too soft.

Preheat the broiler. Cover the broiler pan with aluminum foil. Using a very sharp knife slice the tomatoes paper thin in vertical slices. Lay the slices on the broiler pan (you may have to do this in two batches if they don't fit all at once). In a small bowl mix the olive oil and garlic; brush on the tomato slices. Sprinkle the salt and cracked pepper on top. Broil 4 inches from the heat for about 5 minutes or until browned on the edges and soft. Remove from the heat. Prepare your favorite pasta according to package directions. Drain. In a large pasta serving bowl, place the broiled tomatoes and basil. Pour the pasta on top and stir to coat using two large spoons. Add a little more olive oil if you like. Makes enough sauce for 4 servings of pasta.

Bouillabaisse

This dish is a fancy fish stew. The delicate saffron flavor balances the tomatoes nicely. Serve this hearty dish with a green salad and some crusty bread for a complete meal.

¼	cup olive oil
¼	cup chopped onion
½	teaspoon garlic
2	medium tomatoes, chopped
1	11.5-ounce can tomato juice
2	teaspoons lemon juice
2	cups water
⅛	teaspoon saffron powder or one pinch of saffron threads
1	cup diced peeled potatoes
2	pounds assorted fresh fish (snapper, halibut, scallops, sea bass)
	Salt and pepper to taste

In a soup pot heat the olive oil and brown the onion and garlic. Add the tomatoes, tomato juice, lemon juice, water, saffron, and potatoes. Reduce the heat to medium and simmer for 20 minutes or until the potatoes are cooked through. Cut the fish into 2-inch pieces and add to the soup. Simmer for 10 more minutes, just until the fish is cooked through. Add salt and pepper to taste and serve. Makes 6 to 8 servings.

Also uses potatoes

A lot of recipes that call for tomatoes require that they be peeled and seeded first. That means dipping the tomatoes in boiling water, removing the peels, cutting them in half, removing the seeds, and then chopping the tomatoes. It's very time-consuming, and chances are the tomatoes that you want to use up may break up if you drop them in boiling water. So, plan for using up tomatoes in recipes where the tomatoes don't have to be peeled. For most soup recipes, the tomatoes really don't need to be peeled, and the peels actually add more flavor to the soup. When you're using up tomatoes, you'll probably want to put them in dishes that require cooking rather than mixing in tomatoes without cooking. If they're starting to get a little mushy, they won't have as much flavor if left uncooked. Tomatoes can be used to make a sauce for meats, poultry, fish, or pasta. Tomatoes are also a good ingredient for stews. The pungent and tart flavor of tomatoes balances well with ingredients that are more delicate or sweet, such as onions, carrots, and celery. Tomatoes can also be added as an extra vegetable to mixed vegetable dishes.

2 for — For more recipes that use up tomatoes, see:

Caponata, p. 110
Ratatouille Sandwiches, p. 119
Baja Soup, p. 172
Cha Cha Chili, p. 179
Napa Pasta Sauce, p. 196

NOTES

_____

_____

_____

_____

_____

From the kitchen of ⎯⎯⎯⎯⎯⎯⎯⎯

From the kitchen of ⎯⎯⎯⎯⎯⎯⎯⎯

25
Wine

Ah, vino . . . the perfect accompaniment to any meal until it's over, and then what do you do with the rest? Red wine keeps longer than white wine, but if it's refrigerated, it loses its flavor. Re-corking devices can help extend wine a few days longer. Obviously, it's best to try to use up the wine before it starts turning to vinegar. Fizzy wine like champagne goes flat pretty quickly, but champagne makes a wonderful marinade, especially for delicate foods like fish. Cooking with the same wine you drink, rather than buying a cheaper cooking wine, provides a balance of flavors between the meal and the wine served with it. Wine can add a whole new dimension to cooking. Because it is a fermented product, it's great as a pungent marinade for meats, poultry, and fish. Wine is wonderful in sauces and soups, also. So, one sip for the cook and another for the pot. Enjoy cooking with wine.

Champagne Roast Salmon

Salmon can be prepared in so many different ways: grilling, braising, steaming, broiling, and roasting. It's delicious on its own with no seasoning, and a little bit of flavor goes a long way. Marinating salmon briefly in champagne and roasting it in the oven or on the barbecue is a marvelous way to cook it. It's juicy, delicate, and just delicious.

1   3-pound salmon roast, or 4 thick salmon steaks
Salt and pepper to taste
1   whole onion, thinly sliced horizontally
1   whole lemon, thinly sliced
1   cup champagne (can be flat)
Olive oil

Wash and dry the salmon roast and place in a glass dish. Sprinkle salt and pepper to taste inside the cavity. (If using steaks, sprinkle on both sides.) Inside the cavity (or in between the steaks) place the onion slices and lemon slices. Pour the champagne over and marinate at room temperature for 30 minutes.

Preheat the oven to 400°, or prepare the barbecue grill for medium high heat. Tear off 2 very large sheets of heavy-duty aluminum foil. Place the roast in the center of the first sheet. Pour ¼ cup of marinade from the dish over the salmon. Drizzle with olive oil. Fold up the sides of the foil, then fold and roll down the remaining edges to form a tight packet. Place the packet seam-side down on the second sheet of foil and repeat to form a tight packet around the first. Cook on the prepared grill or in the oven for 30 minutes. Makes 4 to 6 servings.

Also uses lemons and onions

1   tablespoon olive oil
½   medium onion,
    chopped
6   cloves garlic, minced
½   cup chopped fresh basil
    (or 1 teaspoon dried)
6   cremini (brown)
    mushrooms, sliced thin
1   teaspoon dried fennel
    seed
1   teaspoon oregano
    Cracked pepper
3   to 4 cups chopped
    tomatoes (or 2 14-
    ounce cans)
½   cup wine
½   cup water

Napa Pasta Sauce

Everybody has their own favorite pasta sauce, and this one is mine. When my garden tomatoes are in season, I use them in this recipe. Canned tomatoes also work just fine. You can use red or white wine for this recipe, but red wine will give the sauce a more robust flavor.

In a large frying pan or braising pan heat the olive oil and sauté the onion and garlic over medium high heat until soft. Add the basil, mushrooms, fennel, oregano, and a little cracked pepper. Continue to sauté until you can smell the aroma from the herbs. Add the tomatoes, wine, and water. Reduce the heat to low and simmer for 30 to 45 minutes. Makes enough sauce for 4 large servings of pasta.

Also uses tomatoes

Chicken Mushroom Picatta

Picatta is traditionally made with lemon juice and capers. This recipe uses wine in place of lemon. Broth is then added to dilute the wine's pungency a little. Because the chicken is dredged in flour, the sauce thickens automatically. Elegant and easy.

½ cup all-purpose flour
  Salt and pepper to taste
4 skinless, boneless chicken breast halves
2 tablespoons olive oil, divided
2 cups sliced mushrooms
½ cup white wine
½ cup chicken broth
2 tablespoons capers
  Chopped parsley for garnish

On a paper plate mix together the flour, salt, and pepper, and blend with a fork. Wash and dry the chicken breasts and dredge both sides in the flour mixture. In a large skillet or braising pan heat 1 tablespoon olive oil and sauté the mushrooms until golden brown. Remove from the pan and set aside. Add the other 1 tablespoon olive oil to the pan and sauté the chicken breasts on both sides until golden brown over medium high heat. Add the wine and broth, cover the skillet, reduce the heat to medium, and let cook for 15 minutes. Remove the cover and let the sauce thicken a little. Test the chicken to make sure it's cooked through (if not, cover and cook a little longer). Add the capers and mushrooms to the pan and stir to blend the flavors. Place the chicken breasts on a platter; spoon the mushrooms and sauce on top, and sprinkle with parsley. Makes 4 servings.

1   cup red wine
½   cup jam (any flavor)
2   cloves garlic, minced
½   teaspoon dried thyme
½   teaspoon dried oregano
2   tablespoons olive oil
12 whole button
    mushrooms
8   summer squash, cut
    into 1-inch slices
1   pound boneless pork,
    cut into cubes

Barbecue Pork Kebabs

Wine is a wonderful marinade for pork, especially if other spices or sweet ingredients are used. The same marinade also tastes great on traditional kebab vegetables such as squash or mushrooms.

In a blender combine the wine, jam, garlic, herbs, and olive oil. Blend until smooth. Reserve ½ cup of the marinade to use for brushing the kebabs on the grill. In a glass dish combine the mushrooms, squash, and pork, and pour the marinade over. Marinate in the refrigerator for at least 4 hours. Thread the pork and vegetables onto skewers and cook on a barbecue grill over high heat for 15 to 20 minutes or until the pork is cooked through. Makes 4 servings.

Also uses jam

Poached Pears

This is an easy and elegant way to serve pears, and the flavor of the wine enhances the natural sweetness of the fruit. There are many pear varieties to choose from, but I don't care for the Bosc variety because it takes much longer to cook. You can serve them in crystal dessert dishes for an elegant presentation, or serve them over a scoop of vanilla ice cream.

3	ripe but firm pears (Anjou, Bartlett or Comice)
1	cup white wine
¼	cup sugar
1	teaspoon vanilla
½	teaspoon cinnamon

Peel the pears, cut them in half, and remove the core and seeds. In a covered braising pan place the wine, sugar, vanilla, and cinnamon. Bring to a simmer. Place the pears flat side down in the pan and spoon some of the liquid over them. Cover and steam on low for 10 minutes. Turn the pears over and simmer for 10 more minutes or until done. Cool in the pan, then transfer to a glass dish and pour pan syrup over them. Serve warm or chilled. Makes 6 servings.

For more recipes that use up wine, see:

BBQ Beef Ribs, p. 85

Wine's pungency will add tartness to a dish, so make sure that the food can withstand the intense flavor. Some delicate fish such as sole or orange roughy can be overwhelmed with too much wine; a little goes a long way when you're adding wine to fish. Using wine as a marinade base and adding spices and herbs is a wonderful way to introduce flavors and soften the texture of meats or poultry before cooking. Wine can often be used interchangeably with broth in a recipe, but start by replacing just some of the broth, and then add more after tasting. The chicken picatta dish is an example; you need an equal amount of broth and wine. Otherwise, the chicken will have a "pickled" taste.

NOTES

From the kitchen of _____

From the kitchen of _____

⌒ Appendix: Food Storage Guidelines ⌒

CAUTION: USE COMMON SENSE AND PRACTICE FOOD SAFETY

It's one thing to use up ingredients, but by all means don't use these things if the food has spoiled. The best guide is to use your nose first, and then your eyes. If it smells rotten or sour or toxic, throw it away. If it looks moldy or has unidentifiable organisms growing on it (particularly anything that moves!)—throw it out. The idea is to use up things before they spoil—like within a day or two for most ingredients in this book. Many foods are packaged with expiration dates on them, including canned goods. You should refer to these dates and use them as a guide to be absolutely safe. For fresh produce and other items that don't have dates, make a habit of jotting down the date you purchased them, or keep your grocery store register receipts handy, which list the items and the date. Before you start cooking with the ingredients in this book, consult this listing.

These are the safe lengths of time for keeping foods before you should throw them away:

Applesauce
Opened jar or can: one week
Unopened jar or can: 12 months

Bananas
3 to 5 days at room temperature

Bread
2 to 4 days at room temperature
7 to 14 days in the refrigerator

Buttermilk
2 weeks in the refrigerator

Carrots
1 to 2 weeks in the refrigerator

Celery
1 to 2 weeks in the crisper of the refrigerator

Cheese
1 month in the refrigerator; cut off any mold

Chicken
3 to 4 days in the refrigerator

Eggs
Whole eggs: 1 week in the refrigerator
Yolks: 1 to 2 days in the refrigerator
Whites: several weeks in the refrigerator

Honey
12 months stored anywhere

Jam/Jelly
12 months unopened, or 12 months opened in the refrigerator

Lemons
2 weeks stored anywhere

Milk
Opened: 1 week in the refrigerator
Unopened: 30 days in the refrigerator

Olives
Opened: 1 to 2 months in the refrigerator

Onions
2 weeks at room temperature

Orange Juice (Purchased Refrigerated)
Unopened: 3 weeks after expiration date
Opened: 7 to 10 days in the refrigerator

Peas (Frozen)
8 months in the freezer

Potatoes
2 weeks at room temperature

Raisins
6 months to 1 year stored anywhere

Rice (cooked)
3 to 5 days in the refrigerator

Salad Dressing
Unopened: 10 to 12 months at room temperature
Opened: 3 months in the refrigerator

Salsa (fresh-cut)
3 days in the refrigerator

Tomato Paste
Opened: 5 days in the refrigerator

Tomatoes
1 to 2 days in the refrigerator

Wine
A matter of personal taste. Most people say that recorked white wine keeps for 2 or 3 days in the refrigerator; red wine for 3 to 5 days at room temperature or refrigerated. A vacuum pump stopper such as a "Vacu-vin" can extend that by 2 days. After this point, the wine will begin to taste like vinegar, at which point it still can be used as a marinade or in salad dressing.

ADDITIONAL INFORMATION ONLINE

There are several helpful websites about safe food handling that have been developed by the USDA Extension Service, in conjunction with states and other organizations. Here are two of the most comprehensive sites that I found on the Internet. These websites have safe food storage guidelines for almost every type of food imaginable, so you will find it all here. The only thing not included is wine, but there are many websites for wine enthusiasts that also have wine storage tips; just key in search terms "wine storage" and you will find many of them.

1. The Food Keeper: A Consumer Guide to Food Quality and Safe Handling:
    http://www.fmi.org/consumer/foodkeeper/foodkeeper.pdf
    Divided into sections according to how food is purchased (fresh, refrigerated, on the shelf, canned, etc.). Very comprehensive and easy to read lists.

2. Arizona Department of Health Services, Food Safety and Environmental Services, Safe Food Storage Times and Temperatures:
    http://www.hs.state.az.us/phs/oeh/fses/sfstt.htm
    Also a fairly comprehensive guide, this site is divided into several other pages by category of food. It also includes storage temperatures in addition to storage times.

Where to Find 2fer and 3fer Recipes

Index

ᴄ About the Author ᴐ

Catherine Kitcho is an author, publisher, business consultant, and the former owner of a catering company, Five Star Kitchens. Her recipes and food articles have been published online (www.pelepubs.com) and in periodicals. She and her husband live in Mountain View, California, where her tiny but productive vegetable garden keeps her busy using up tomatoes, potatoes, carrots, and onions.